The Leader's Motivation

Bob Gordon

with David Fardouly

Sovereign World

Sovereign World
PO Box 777
Tonbridge
Kent TN11 0ZS
England

All Bible quotations are taken from the New International Version of the
Holy Bible, copyright © 1973, 1978 International Bible Society,
published by Hodder and Stoughton, unless otherwise stated.
Quotations marked AV are taken from the Authorised Version, Crown
copyright.

NKJV – New King James Bible © Thomas Nelson Publishers Inc,
PO Box 141000, Nashville, TN 37214, USA.

RSV – Revised Standard Version, copyright © Churches of Christ in the
United States of America.

NASB – New American Standard Bible, copyright © The Lockman
Foundation 1960, 1962, 1963, 1968, 1971, 1973, 1977.

Living Bible. Copyright © 1971 Tyndale House Publishers, Wheaton,
Illinois 60187 USA.

Amplified Bible. Copyright © 1965, Zondervan Publishing House, Grand
Rapids, Michigan MI 49506 USA.

The New Testament in Modern English. Copyright © 1958 by
J.B. Phillips, The Macmillan Company, Collins, London, UK.

ISBN 1 85240 262 8

This Sovereign World book is distributed in North America by Renew
Books, a ministry of Gospel Light, Ventura, California, USA. For a free
catalog of resources from Renew Books/Gospel Light, please contact your
Christian supplier or call 1-800-4-GOSPEL.

Typeset by CRB Associates, Reepham, Norfolk.
Printed in England by Clays Ltd, St Ives plc.

Contents

A Living Legacy

'He being dead still speaks.'   (Hebrews 11:4)

When Bob went to be with the Lord in September 1997, I was left with a huge chasm in my life and a deep sense of sadness and loss. Not only had I lost a husband, a friend, a lover, and a father for Jonathan, but also my *'father in God'* (1 Corinthians 4:15).

However, amongst all the questions and confusion in my heart at that time, there was one thing of which I was certain – that Bob had left the Body of Christ a 'Living Legacy' through his writings. So, spurred on by the Holy Spirit and whatever else it takes, I mean to keep those books available.

The *Master Builders* series is a set of books on leadership, a subject in which Bob was keenly involved; so much so that he established the Proclaimers Network and the Proclaimers Forum for the refreshment, encouragement and building up of men and women of God in the forefront of leadership. His great partner and friend in this was Derek Brown, and I would therefore like to dedicate this new series to Derek who is in the same 'apostolic' line as Bob of the 'fathers in God' we have in this nation.

I would like to thank Angie Hindmarsh for her tremendous help, support and friendship in this venture; my dear friend, Ann Thomas, who proof read the script and has been an enormous support to me over the past two years; and to the staff of Sovereign World, particularly Chris and Jan Mungeam for their personal love, encouragement and tireless work in bringing about the new *Master Builders* series.

Hilda Gordon
June 1999

Introduction

'According to the grace of God which was given to me, as a wise master builder I have laid the foundation, and another builds on it. But let each one take heed how he builds on it. For no other foundation con anyone lay than that which is laid, which is Jesus Christ.' (1 Corinthians 3:10, 11 NKJV)

Master Builders is offered as a study guide to encourage maturity and growth within Christian leadership today. The subject has always been high on God's agenda, since people cannot function without proper leadership. In those days when the ancient people of God found themselves without true leadership, chaos and anarchy ruled even in their ranks. The cry of the book of Judges echoes this reality:

'In those days there was no king in Israel; everyone did what was right in his own eyes.' (Judges 17:6 NKJV)

Whether in the world at large or in the Church in particular, anointed and godly leadership is crucial.

Most of the credit for the shape of this particular book must go to my colleague David Fardouly, who has brought together a great deal of my own teaching from a wide variety of sources, spiced it with additions and illustrations from the work of others.

Four basic convictions underlie this work:

1. That there is a desperate need for true leadership and maturity in the body of Christ at this time. A good foundation is necessary if we are to be capable witnesses to the gospel in our generation.

2. That we need to underline the responsibility each of us faces if we are to grow in gift and ministry. It is important to dispel the myth among Christians that all out needs will continually fall from the sky. It is not so, much application and hard work is called for if excellence is to be achieved amongst God's people.

3. That growth is a corporate business. Paul once said that we have many guardians in Christ, but few fathers (1 Corinthians 4:15). We all need spiritual fatherhood, because that is what sets the example and provides the stimulus for each one of us to progress in spiritual things. We need to learn from each other. This book is offered as a learning experience. You may not agree with everything in it and at best it is only partial, but perhaps it can serve as a catalyst to thought and action that will lead to growth.

4. That a balanced view of leadership is necessary. Leaders are not called to lord it over God's people. Neither are God's people called to be free democrats. Both extremes seem to have reared their heads in recent years. We have tried to present a clear, practical and spiritual challenge to all who desire to grow in spiritual responsibility.

Many others also deserve recognition for their practical help and guidance in putting this series of books together – particularly Pete Goddard and Nicci Gagel for her whole-hearted efforts in compiling the text. Finally, I would want to thank Chris Mungeam and the staff of Sovereign World Limited, who have shown no limits in their support for our work and ministry.

Bob Gordon

Chapter 1

Principles of Motivation

> ***Nothing gets done without motivation.***

Introduction

Why is it that on some days we would climb the highest
mountains and swim the widest oceans for the Lord, and yet
on other days we can hardly manage to lift a finger for Him?
What induces us to serve the Lord anyway? How on earth do
we serve the Lord wholeheartedly as we know we should?
How do we get other people to serve the Lord wholeheartedly? In the next few chapters, we will be looking at the
whole concept of motivation. It is hoped that by the time
you finish reading them, you will adequately be able to
answer these questions and others like them.

Motivation defined

Motivation can be defined as that which initiates motion or
that which induces a person to act. It is human energy,
which is probably the most plentiful and powerful resource
on earth. We can never run out of it, and yet it always seems
to be lacking or worse still, badly directed. The list of things
that can motivate us is endless. This list will vary from
person to person and will even vary from day to day. The

following table lists some of the things that motivate us as Christians:

Negative	Neutral	Positive
Compulsion	Happiness	Godliness
Anger	Honour	Holiness
Jealousy	Euphoria	Righteousness
Hurts	Satisfaction	Peace
Fear	Compromise	Joy
Pride	Disagreement	Kindness
Laziness	Pressure	Goodness
Hatred	Cleanliness	Faithfulness
Envy	Desire	Mercy
Loneliness	Circumstances	Hope
Evil	Good Will	Love
Despair	Morality	Selflessness
Insecurity	Security	Fear of God
Complacency	Competition	Patience
Worry	Excitement	Gentleness
Guilt	Pleasure	Self-control
Discouragement	Conscience	Vision from God
Deceit	Success	Grace
Disappointment	Physical fitness	God-consciousness

This list is in no particular order, and an entry in one column could, in certain circumstances, be placed in another. The list is given only to give you an idea of the quantity and variety of the sources of motivation (and there are many others that we could add to it).

Throughout the rest of this chapter, we will examine the principles of motivation; and in the following two chapters, we will look at the things that God wants, and does not want, to motivate us as we serve Him. We start with the principles of motivation, because it is helpful to understand how motivation works and what effect it can have on our lives. Our understanding of motivation can make the difference between having a ministry which is effective, and one which does not seem able to get off the ground. This important topic needs to be looked at in some detail.

Three basic sources of human motivation

1. Probably the most powerful, and yet the most basic source of human motivation we all have, is for survival. This needs to be realised, because if we are trying to do anything to help a person whose survival is threatened (e.g. by hunger, disease, even old age, etc.), we will have to take into account that this is probably dominating their thinking and motivating most of their actions.

2. Another basic source of human motivation which needs to be understood is that all people want to make sense of life, have a purpose, and make their lives count for something. This is because God created all human beings with an inbuilt need to know Him and do His will. This source of motivation may be largely an unconscious drive in some, but it is the source of motivation behind all religions, including atheism.

3. The third basic source of human motivation which operates within all of us, including Christians, is the powerful drive to only do things which are good for us. This selfish or self-centred source of motivation pushes us to put ourselves as the priority in our lives and so it must be taken into account.

As Christians, we need to put God first in everything. This will mean that we have to deny ourselves, something which does not come naturally to a human being. However, in Christ such a life is possible. We need to give God the Lordship of all of our life and, therefore, seek to live obedient, selfless lives in which God and His will takes precedence over ourselves and our will (Luke 9:23). Outside of God, people gain meaning from: accomplishing worthwhile tasks; achieving goals and completing jobs that they have started; meeting self-imposed standards; developing satisfying relationships with other people; exercising power over and manipulating other people, and so to some extent being instrumental in changing those people and the world; and making enough money to get the things they need and want in life. Christians also have these sources of motivation operating to some extent in their lives, but God wants us to be different. As Christians, we need to understand what motivates us and, further, we need to know how to stay motivated 100% of the time by the right things, so that we can serve our Lord effectively and fruitfully. Our purpose and meaning and, therefore, our life should revolve around God and our relationship with Him. Everything we do should be because He wants it and because we love Him.

What are motivated people like?

Motivated people are first and foremost, willing people. A good example of a willing group of people can be seen when the children of Israel brought their offerings for the building of the tabernacle of the Lord (Exodus 35:4–36:7). Here the people had to be restrained from bringing more, because they were so willing to give. Many leaders would probably want such a problem in their church! Why is it that these people were so willing? The answer is simply that God and His work had captivated the hearts of these people, and so they stopped grumbling, and instead, became willing, motivated people.

Motivated people also want to get the job done. Their motivation encourages them into action. The stronger the motivation, the more sacrificial of time, money and energy, they will be. In fact, highly motivated people will be determined to get the job done, even in the face of strong opposition. They are, therefore, usually people who achieve much in life.

There are many characteristics that we could associate with a highly motivated person. In the list below, we have sought to select some of the most commonly seen characteristics in high achieving, highly motivated Christians. These are characteristics which any Christian who wants to serve the Lord more effectively, should develop.

- They have got themselves in hand and live a disciplined, godly life which seeks to put God and His will first. They set goals for their life and plan strategies to achieve them that they stick to (when possible) until the job gets done. In fact, they seek to excel in everything they do for God. They do not wear themselves out and they are not lazy, because they have achieved a balance in life which enables them to live purposefully and productively. They also make sure that they do not neglect any area of their life. They, therefore, allow time for their physical, emotional, intellectual, social and spiritual needs to be met. They also know how to be angry and sin not (Ephesians 4:26 NKJV). Like Jesus, they have a righteous anger towards sin, hypocrisy and injustice, but they know how to control their temper. In fact, they do not let the sun go down on their anger towards another person without first forgiving them, because they know that the bitterness and grudge-bearing which would result outside of forgiveness would destroy their motivation and their effectiveness for God (Ephesians 4:26, 27; James 1:19, 20).

- They have an optimistic approach to life, believing that all problems are solvable in God. They may be discouraged at times, but generally they are not depressed or down. Whereas the pessimist sees difficulty in every opportunity, the optimist sees opportunity in every difficulty. They are therefore willing to tackle the tough jobs. They also live a happy, fulfilling life, because they are willing to work at this and be creative (use their imagination) in what they do with their time and effort. They are also open/alert/receptive, and interested in people, new ideas, and knowledge.

- They may or may not be visionaries, but they have a sense of direction for their lives, and can catch a hold of the vision of God and run with it. They are often persuasive people who can sell their ideas to others. They are always looking ahead to see results and, therefore, they have the insight/discernment to make good decisions. They are also practical, in that they know vision has to be translated into reality.

- They are willing to stretch themselves to their limit in mind and body as they seek to fulfil the will of God; they are willing to step out in faith and take risks when necessary; and they are capable of change and being versatile when they need to be.

- They are full of confidence in God and what He can do through them. They know that if they cannot believe in themselves, no one else will believe in them either. Their confidence enables them to laugh at themselves when they get it wrong or when things go wrong. Their confidence in God also gives them courage. They are determined, enthusiastic, persistent, and they do not give up unless they realise they have got it wrong in God. They know that God is with them, and so even when they are afraid, they push on and refuse to let their fear overcome and defeat them (Joshua 1:1–9).

- They are humble, knowing that it is God who deserves the credit and the glory for their success. They do not need to boast about their achievements and success, because these speak for themselves.

- They are patient, knowing that God always proves faithful, but that He has a time for everything (Ecclesiastes 3:1–8). They are also good listeners and good communicators, and they only make important decisions after they have gathered enough relevant information.

- They are trustworthy, because they live a life of integrity/honesty and they understand responsibility. Their word means something and they can be counted on, especially when the going gets tough. Above all, they refuse to cheat in any area of their life, because they know that this may make things easier in the short-term, but they will not be able to live with themselves.

Our world today

The world around us is becoming increasingly competitive and less predictable with each day that passes. The human race has entered the atomic age, the space age, and the computer age in the last 50 years. It has been calculated that people entering the workforce, on average, will have to understand over 20 times as much information as they would just one generation ago.

Christians are not exempt from this phenomenon. We have to live in the world and to some extent be a part of it. Most of us have to work for a living in the market place, and we can so easily be caught up in the whirl-wind of activity around us at the cost of our walk with God. Church leaders today have to make a huge number of choices, e.g. what to read (out of the mountain of books available); what teaching to believe and make their own, and what to teach their people (out of the increase in variety and amount of teaching which is competing for our time and money); what seminars to attend; how many meetings to have in our church and which ones to attend, etc. Church members today are also becoming far more demanding of their leaders and what they expect from them. The instant, high-pressure, result-oriented world in which we live is encroaching into the church and bringing with it all the problems and sometimes also the enabling of success that this entails.

Church leaders need to negotiate this mine-field and stay motivated in their service for God as they do. Today's western world is not an easy environment in which to live a good, effective Christian life which brings glory to God, but it is possible to do so. In order to do this, we need to learn about ourselves and who we are in God. We also need to know how we react to different situations and circumstances, and why. Most importantly, we need to make ourselves totally available to God so that He can change and equip us where necessary. Only then will we be truly ready and able to carry out His will in His way. God wants His leaders to be highly motivated and, therefore, fruitful and effective for Him wherever they live and whatever they are doing.

The three ways people react to pressure

The change in the pace of the world today, the growth of readily available information, and the demand for better performance, even in Christian circles, all cause us to have to cope with vastly increased amounts of pressure. It is therefore helpful to understand how we as people react to pressure. Here we will concentrate on the effect pressure can have on our motivation. It has been found that there are basically three ways people respond to pressure. The following categories describe them:

1. The tail-chaser

These people take on more and speed up in response to pressure. As a result, they are often driven, hyperactive and aggressive people. We have labelled this group 'tail-chasers', because they behave like a dog chasing its tail, i.e. they rush frantically around in circles trying to reach their goal. If they do manage to achieve what they set out to do, they often do not know what to do with themselves, until they find the next thing they can madly chase after, i.e. they see that tail again and want it at all costs.

Such a person usually rushes around and tries to do too much, too quickly and, as a result, accomplishes very little of quality. They tend to take on too many responsibilities and they over-commit and over-challenge themselves. Time is the enemy of these people and they have a sense of urgency and hurriedness about everything they do. They tend to try too hard and take unrealistically high risks in an attempt to get a job done faster. They also often expect a great deal more than is realistic of those who work for them, and even get angry when these people do not live up to their expectations. If things are not done yesterday, they are not happy. These people are also prone to try and take short-cuts to success, and so they cut down on planning time and they do not allow enough time for skill development and mastery. Panic is often the main source of their energy and, because of this, these people tend to be unable to concentrate for any length of time, i.e. they find their minds darting from one thing to another.

The cost of such behaviour is great. Not only are they ineffective, but these people carry with them a huge amount of stress and tension. This encourages frustration, nervousness, anger, physical illness (such as heart disease and cancer), alcoholism, excessive smoking, drug dependence, mental breakdown, and even suicide. To feel out of control of your own life, to feel that you are in way over your head, and to be dictated to and controlled by what is happening around you, is a frightening state to be in.

People who react to pressure by increasing their work-load and speeding up, often spiral downwards, i.e. the more they try to get done and the harder and faster they work, the less they tend to achieve; and the less they achieve, the harder they feel they have to work and the more they will take on. Even if these people do meet with success, all this seems to do is reinforce and encourage their wrong behaviour, i.e. they believe that taking on more work and doing it faster is the only way for them to accomplish anything and be the success that they so desperately want to be. The vicious cycle in which these people are trapped is a never-ending exercise in futility which often results in tragedy.

2. The ostrich

These people ignore, slow down or run from pressure. This response to pressure tends to result in demotivated, care-free, careless people, who are more concerned with them-selves than they are with getting the job done. These people would rather have the pressure disappear, and so they either bury their head in the sand and refuse to admit that the pressure exists; or they turn their backs on the cause or source of the pressure and run away from it, even if it is something that urgently needs to be done. Although these people may not have as high blood-pressure as those in the first group, they tend to live lives that lack excitement and enthusiasm. They generally are not high achievers, because they do not have the motivation and drive needed to take the necessary risks and overcome the inevitable challenges involved. Their lethargic, safety-at-all-cost attitude causes them to be safe, but sorry. When these people reluctantly take on pressure, they do so half-heartedly, expecting and, therefore, insuring poor performance. This then reinforces the person's dislike of pressure situations and causes them to try and avoid or run away from such situations with more tenacity next time.

The greatest cost of such behaviour is that these people feel their life is going no-where. They are often bored, and have a dislike for or little interest in their job. These people are usually at least competent at what they do, but they do not want to go beyond their area of competence and step out into new areas, i.e. do things they have never done before, or go beyond where they have been before. To step out into some new area of endeavour is seen by them as too risky, mainly because of the fear of failure. Life, therefore, is rather too predictable and routine for these people and so they readily lose interest in what they are doing, preferring to 'jog' along and do enough to keep everybody happy. These people often risk the depression-based illnesses due to their frustration, depression, lack of fulfilment, disillusionment, and disappointment.

3. The ideal

This group responds to pressure in the ideal way, i.e. they allow it to motivate them to perform at their peak and so get the necessary jobs done. We have looked at this in an earlier chapter, so we will not look at this response to pressure in much detail. Suffice to say here that these people do not allow their circumstances to dictate to or control them. They take on stress, but they also know how to channel it, instead of absorbing it into themselves and therefore suffering from it. They tend to be committed to their work and confidently take the risks involved necessary to do their job, without being unrealistic and therefore overwhelmed by what they are doing. Basically, they are in control of themselves and their situation, and they either have (or are in the process of being trained in order to have), the necessary skills to do their job in the most effective way possible. Of course, this is an ideal situation. Sometimes, it is not possible to have further training and we simply have to make do. At other times, we have to take on things which leave us feeling we are way out of our depth, and yet, as Christians, we can know God's enabling to offset our weakness.

Of course, we all react differently to the different tasks and challenges that come our way throughout life. These three descriptions are given simply to help each one of us know how we are reacting to the pressure accompanying the situations we encounter in life. The ideal response to pressure is the response for which we should all be aiming as Christians, so that we can maximise our effectiveness and achieve the best possible results for God.

The balance between skill, God-given gifting and attitude

Performing at our best as a Christian is a combination of skill, God-given gifting and attitude. Skill can be defined as having the knowledge and the ability to do something. As a rule, this is necessary before we can tackle any activity successfully. God has also promised that He will provide us with everything we need for life and godliness (2 Peter 1:3), as long as we submit our lives to His will. To know God's gifting is essential, if we want to serve Him effectively as Christians. However, although these two things are obviously very important, it is attitude that sets apart those who are going to be really successful from those who will simply be adequate. Skills, and even the gifting of God, are possessed by many, but only a few Christians are really successful for God. This is partly due to the different call which God places on our lives, i.e. some are called to greatness and to achieve much, and some are called to simply keep things going. However, it is also true that many Christians have the potential to do much for God, and yet fail to get their act together and so are only partially successful. The thing that makes the difference is usually their attitude.

Attitude may be defined as thinking, outlook or perspective which motivates or disposes us to act in a certain way. Our attitude is controlled or harnessed effectively by only a few of us. It is our attitude that determines how well we use our skills and God-given gifting, and it even determines how well we express or use what we know intellectually. Our attitude influences our perception of any situation, i.e. it determines how we are going to view it; and it also determines how well we are going to perform in that situation.

It is very easy for an attitude problem to reap havoc in our life. This is because it can cause us not only to do badly in one situation, but to do badly in every situation we encounter. For example, a common attitude problem is an expectation of failure. This usually arises because of a past failure which causes us to feel badly about ourselves. This attitude is then carried into other things that we do and it causes us to fail there also. To be caught in such a cycle will cause us to continually perform poorly. Christians trapped in a vicious cycle like this (in which they are going from bad to worse), need to break out, if they are ever going to be effective and successful for God. To do this, they will need to get help from God and other people. Simply to think positively is not the answer. The root cause of the problem needs to be dealt with, i.e. their attitude problem needs to be rectified.

What we need to do, as Christians, is to go from good to better. If we are successful in what we do, because we see ourselves as God sees us and, therefore, have a good self-image; if we are skilled and competent enough to be realistically confident (in both God and our gifting) in any situation; if we are committed to what we are doing because we know it is God's will for us at that time; and if we (with God) are in control of the situation; then it should be possible to be continually highly motivated and successful in nearly everything we do. Being successful will reinforce our right attitude and behaviour and enable us to continue it.

The following are some helpful thoughts to enable us to keep the right attitude in our service for God.

- We need to assess our results and learn any lessons possible from these. There are many questions we could ask ourselves. What we learn from answering these can be applied to the next situation we encounter and enable us to go from good to better in our service for God. Some questions we could ask ourselves include:

- Were my skills adequate for the task?
- How could I improve my performance?
- What things prevented me from doing any better?
- What would I have done if given the task again?
- Did I bring God into the situation?
- Did I know God with me as I did my job?
- How accurately did I perceive the situation?
- Did I believe I would be successful?
- How did I feel about myself and my ability to cope?

- Our attitude toward life will determine how we get on in life. We need to accept ourselves as Christians, knowing that God loves us and has chosen us. He knows what attitudes we harbour in our hearts (Hebrews 4:12, 13). He knew what we would be like physically, emotionally and intellectually, and He has gifted us in a unique way so that we have the potential to do something for Him that no one else could do quite as well. God is able to use us as we are, but He wants us to progress and grow in maturity in Him so that He can use us even more in His service. We need to put off our old self, which is being corrupted by its deceitful desires; and allow God to make us new in the attitude of our minds; and we need to put on our new self in Christ, which is created to be like God in true righteousness and holiness (Ephesians 4:22–24).

- We need to think, act, and talk in ways characteristic of who we ultimately wish to become, i.e. as Christians, we need to think, act and talk like Jesus (Philippians 2:5–11; 1 Peter 4:1, 2).

- Our attitude toward other people will determine their attitude toward us, e.g. if we always make other people feel needed, important and appreciated, they will return this attitude to us. Do unto others as you would have them do unto you; and treat everyone with respect, dignity and courtesy, where possible. It is also not a good idea to talk about your health (unless it is good), or your personal problems (as it probably will not help you and certainly will not help other people).

- Our attitude at the beginning of a task will effect our performance during and the outcome of that task.

- We need to be creative, look for new ideas everywhere, and find the best in them.

- We must not be embarrassed to share vision, desires and goals.

- When we really want to do God's will and we are committed to seeing it through, our attitude will be right.

- We should radiate an attitude of well-being and courage. We should be positive, optimistic and think only about what is true, noble, pure, lovely, admirable, excellent, and praise-worthy (Philippians 4:8).

- We need to rid ourselves of our bad habits, deal with our fears, and learn the necessary skills, so that these things no longer block our effectiveness for God.

Commitment and what captivates our heart

Our heart is the seed-bed of our thoughts, attitudes, motives and decisions. The things that captivate our hearts tend to dominate our thoughts and emotions, and influence the decisions of our will (Proverbs 27:19; Proverbs 4:23; Luke 6:43–45). The more our heart is captivated by something, the more we will want or desire it; the more we desire something, the greater our commitment to it will be; and the greater our commitment, the greater our motivation to achieve our desire will be. A captivated heart and the commitment this creates will motivate us to overcome even the greatest of obstacles, and to press on, even when this involves great cost to ourselves. In fact, the more we are committed to something, the less difficult it appears to be. Anything seems possible and nothing is too much trouble. Obstacles are seen as hurdles which must be overcome and setbacks are seen as opportunities to learn (i.e. how not to do it and how to do it better next time). A captivated heart refuses to accept failure and it never gives up. Like the apostle Paul, it presses on towards the goal to win the prize (Philippians 3:12–14; Colossians 3:23, 24).

As Christians, we need to allow God and His work to captivate our heart, so that He and the accomplishment of His will become what we want or desire more than anything else (1 Corinthians 4:5; 2 Thessalonians 3:5; Proverbs 3:5, 6; Psalm 119:1–3). For this to be possible, we need to meet with God and get to know Him and His desires. Then, our heart will begin to beat in tune with His and we will start to become like Him. His will, will become our will. If we allow Him, He will envision us and captivate our heart with some task. He may have to do a work of preparation in our lives before hand, but if we continue to look to Him, He will show us what He wants us to do for Him. A heart captivated by God and His will, will give us the commitment, motivation, energy, and drive to do God's will, whatever the cost. This is what happened to the great characters of the Bible, like Moses and David, and it can also happen to us. People may be able to get us moving temporarily by inspirational speeches or by dangling rewards before us, but nothing can motivate a Christian more than truly meeting with God, understanding His will, and obeying it.

Our heart will be captivated by what we allow ourselves to participate in and by what we input into our lives. Therefore, we must be careful, because even as Christians our hearts can be stolen, if we let down our defence and let the enemy in. If we allow this to happen, it can be devastating to our motivation to serve the Lord. We will begin to commit ourselves to something other than God and His will and, once this happens, our hearts will encourage us to continue in our wrong behaviour (Jeremiah 17:9; Romans 1:21). Some wrong things that can captivate our heart as Christians include: sin (Hebrews 3:12); ourselves (Proverbs 14:10); doubt (and eventually unbelief); fear and worry (Deuteronomy 20:8); other people (Psalm 69:20); depression, rebellion, disillusionment, disappointment, bitterness and hurt.

As God's sons, we must never allow our hearts to become closed to Him, especially during times when we are down or emotionally hurt. God expects us to keep our eyes on Him and to forgive, thus stopping our hearts from becoming like stone to Him. As Christians, God wants us to be totally available to Him at all times. We must, therefore, never allow our hearts to become closed or numb to God, thus prevent Him from captivating them by Himself and the things He wants us to do for Him. We need to be honest with ourselves and with God. After all, we cannot hide our hearts from Him (1 Samuel 16:7). If our hearts are hardened, and we know that we are not right with God, then we need to go to Him, tell Him about it, and yield our lives afresh into His hand. He will create in us a clean heart that is totally open and available for Him to use (Psalm 139:23, 24; Ezekiel 18:31, 32; Psalm 51:10–12).

To maintain a God-captivated heart, we need to: let His peace guard and rule our heart (Philippians 4:7; Colossians 3:15); spend time each day in God's presence and with His Word (1 John 3:19–21; Hebrews 4:12); store up our treasure in heaven (Matthew 6:19–21); maintain a thankful heart and a humble, Christ-like attitude (Psalm 10:17 NKJV; Ephesians 5:19, 20); fear the Lord (Deuteronomy 5:29; Proverbs 28:14); consecrate our hearts to God and allow Him always to reign as Lord in them (Mark 12:29–31); discipline ourselves so that we always chose to do God's will (Galatians 6:9 Living Bible; Proverbs 23:19).

A God-captivated heart, and the commitment to God and His will that this creates, is a very important key to living a fruitful, God-glorifying life. As Christians, we need to decide what we are going to allow to captivate our hearts. We then need to act upon our decision and live a life into which only those things which God wants are input. This may necessitate us giving up some of the things we are currently doing or feeding into ourselves. It may even cause us to become distant from some of our friends. God asks us to live a selfless, righteous, holy life which is totally given over to Him. We should do everything that we do, only because it is what He wants. This will mean making some very costly sacrifices, but none more costly than the sacrifice God made for us in Jesus.

Determination

Someone once wrote, 'Consider the postage stamp, my son. Its usefulness consists in its ability to stick to one thing until it gets there.' People who are successful in any field are usually those people who do not give up. When the difficulties come, and they inevitably will, these people simply move into a higher, more determined gear until they see their way through. They work in order to see results and to achieve. It is not wrong for a Christian to view God's work in this way. Too many of us achieve little, if anything, for our God. Christians should hear from God and then be determined to carry out His will. Nothing should stop us.

Robert Schuller once said, 'Great people are ordinary people with extra-ordinary amounts of determination.' The trouble with many Christians is that they either do not start anything, or they are put off by the first sign of difficulty. We will achieve nothing for God, if this is our attitude. One night after he had given one of the greatest concerts of his brilliant career, Fritz Kreisler was greeted by an over eager fan who said, 'Oh, I'd give my life to be able to play like you do'. Kreisler replied quietly, 'I did!' Christians should be just as determined as he was. God has chosen us to be His ambassadors and to do His work on this earth. We need to be totally committed to whatever He has planned for us to do and be thoroughly determined to see this work through to the end (until everything we can do is complete), whatever the cost to ourselves. In fact, we should give our life to it (1 Corinthians 9:24–27; 1 Timothy 4:16). This may necessitate taking on some very large difficulties, overcoming some of our deficiencies, or paying a huge cost in terms of our money, time and effort; but it is worth it, if we are committed to the right things. We will not get anywhere or achieve anything unless we commit ourselves to something, act on this, and keep going until we have totally outworked our commitment.

Jesus said,

> *'No one who puts his hand to the plough and looks back is fit for service in the kingdom of God.'* (Luke 9:62)

Confidence in ourselves and in God

The major key to success is us and our relationship with God; not our boss, salary, position or anything else. We need to be confident in ourselves and in what God can do through us, in order to be really fruitful and effective for Him. We need to be confident that we can do the job to which we are called by God and we need to see ourselves as He sees us in that job. God has promised to equip us adequately for any task He asks us to do for Him. Our confidence in God and ourselves should not waver when we fail or when other people are not doing what they should be doing. We need to see ourselves and our circumstances, no matter how bad they seem, as God sees them. We can then relax, do our best for God, and commit ourselves fully into any task He asks us to do for Him, knowing that this is all God expects of us. If we have such an attitude, we will feel free to try new things, when appropriate, and be free to change the way we have always done it, if necessary. The confidence we can have in God and ourselves (when we are doing His will!), can be very liberating and a tremendous stimulant to our motivation to serve Him.

If we work purely with human confidence, our actions will be confined within its boundaries. As Christians, we need to work from a confidence based on our position in God and on the knowledge that God can produce divine results through us, if we make ourselves available to Him. Confidence based on these things will not cause us to fall into pride, arrogance or fear, but will enable us to step out in faith and give all the glory and credit to God for any work He does through us (1 Corinthians 4:1–5; 2 Corinthians 3:4–6; 4:7). We do not carry our destiny on our own shoulders alone. God is with us! Our abilities may not be sufficient to do all that we know needs doing, but His are! This should be the source of a Christian's security and confidence.

Fear is the great enemy of confidence, even for many Christians. It can drive us into a panic; cause us to be hasty in our actions; and even stop us working altogether. Christians have been set free from fear (2 Timothy 1:7; John

8:32, 36; Hebrews 2:15), but many still live with it and are made ineffective in their service for God because of it.

Every human being has built into them the capacity to know fear and anxiety. We usually cannot stop fear from happening, but we can learn how to handle it in God. We need to handle fear, because it distorts our perception, making the situation that aroused the fear look more danger-ous and difficult than it really is, and our ability to handle the situation appear diminished. Our imagination runs wild when we are in a state of fear. 'What might happen if...?' Remote improbabilities seem more like realistic probabilities. We also tend only to notice the things that reinforce or increase our fear, thus making the situation appear to be getting worse all the time. Fear also magnifies the conse-quences of failing to horrible, catastrophic dimensions. Another disconcerting aspect of fear is that often you cannot quite put your finger on the exact reason for being afraid.

The two most common reactions to fear are to be immobil-ised by it or to try and fight our way through it, i.e. we over-react! The best way for a Christian to handle fear is to recognise that this is what is happening, and then to stop and confront the fear. To do this, we need to calm down and take the situation to the Lord. Too many Christians simply try to bury their fears and they find that they return at the most inconvenient moments to plague them. Some of the warning signs we can look for to detect a fear response starting include: talking to ourselves in a negative way, (e.g. 'I cannot really do this!' or 'I am going to let them down this time and they are going to be so angry with me!'); or body reactions like shortness of breath, dry mouth, shaky knees, sweaty palms, feeling rising panic, etc. When we recognise some of these fear warning signs, we should stop, and relax by taking a few deep breaths. Calming down and stopping what we are doing (when possible) gives us the chance to distance ourselves from our fear, and it creates a space in which we can evaluate the situation we are in. We can use this space to try and determine what is causing the fear response in us. As Christians, we can also use this space to bring God into the situation, and ask Him what is really happening and why we are reacting as we are. This will enable us to see what is really there and the situation as it really is – we will again be able to distinguish between a molehill and a mountain. Usually a more accurate, calm appraisal of the situation and seeing things as God sees them, will diminish our fear and help us to get back in control of ourselves (2 Kings 6:8–23).

There are some other helpful things we can do in a fear-causing situation. Firstly, we can write a list of everything we need to do on a board or a piece of paper. We should ask God to help us do this. Many of us distort the amount of work we have to do by keeping this list in our head only. Physically looking at this list will help us to see more clearly what is really there to be done and help us to evaluate it better. Secondly, we can try to measure the actual difficulty of the situation confronting us. When our mind is asked to rate something, (e.g. giving it a score out of ten), the mind becomes analytical and objective. This often breaks through the distorted picture the fear has caused us to see. Thirdly, we can assess ourselves. We can ask if we really did hear from the Lord. If so, there is no need to fear, because God will provide for us and enable us to succeed in the situation. If not, we may need to get out of the situation in the best way we can, e.g. if the mountain really is a mountain. We also need to ask if we have been in a similar situation before (even if only part is similar) and make a comparison. If we have coped well in a similar situation, this will encourage us. If we have not coped well, we may need to make a tactical retreat, or seek God for the courage and determination to succeed this time. We should also go to God and make sure we are not stepping out of our depth in Him without His say so; and find out from Him if we are still on the right course or whether we need to adjust what we are doing. The final thing to do is to imagine the worst if we fail. When we realistically decide what the worst possible consequence of failure is in our situation, we can decide whether we can live with this or not. If we can, we can go ahead. Rating the likelihood of this worst conse-quence happening can also help us, because our mind has often exaggerated this and made it seem far more likely to happen than is realistically possible. Unassessed prospects of disaster keeps us from working well.

Never start a job without first assessing it with God's help. Once we have seen things realistically and from God's perspective, we can more easily decide what our next move should be in our situation. Going into a job with false confidence, based on a positive confession, a vague hope, an over-estimation of our ability, or an under-estimation of the difficulty of the situation, could end in disaster. God tells us to be sober in our judgement of ourselves (Romans 12:3). To judge or discern incorrectly can cause us to go into a situation under-prepared, or cause us to be less careful or diligent than we should be. We also need to assess with God whether we need further training and/or more help, in order to carry out a job successfully. To know that we are adequately trained (or competent) to do a job is a tremendous help to going into that job with a confident attitude; and, as we have discovered, having the right attitude at the beginning of a job will vastly increase our likelihood of success.

Tips to help us keep motivated as leaders

- Being recognised and appreciated for what we do. This gives all of us encouragement to continue doing whatever caused someone to affirm us. We all need to have someone tell us that we are getting somewhere when we have put a lot of effort into doing just that. We also need to be accepted by other people; and to accept/ respect ourselves and our own worth in God, if we are going to stay motivated.

- Knowing that we are called to the task of leadership by God, because then we will know that He is in it with us. This will give us the security and the peace of God that we need in order to maintain our motivation to serve the Lord as one of His leaders.

- Seeking to a be a model for those we lead. This will help motivate us to do the right thing and to continue to live a righteous, holy life; and it will inspire those we lead to do the same.

- Not focusing our attention on things which are outside our control and worrying about these things. This simply tends to waste our time and energy, and sap our motivation. For example, we cannot control another person's needs, attitudes or responses to any great degree. We may be able to influence their actions (especially by prayer), but influence is a long way from control. We are ultimately only really responsible before God for ourselves and what we do.

- Giving to or sharing with other people. God often pours back into our life more than we give out, so that we can give again (Luke 6:38; 2 Corinthians 9:6). Of course, giving involves more than finances. It covers areas like love, happiness, encouragement, time, friendship, and practical help. We can wish and dream all we want, but in the end, we reap what we sow. If you do not like what you see in your life, check what you are sowing into it.

- Knowing that we are working together with other people to achieve commonly held goals and objectives. This can give us a tremendous boost to our motivation. It helps us to feel involved, important, needed and purposeful. Achievement also seems to mean more when other people can share in it.

- Knowing that we are accountable before God for our life and our talent. This encourages us to be productive and fruitful for God. We can also help ourselves in this area by being accountable to the right group of friends with whom we share our lives, i.e. the victories, as well as the failures.

- Never putting off what we know we should do. Success-ful, highly motivated people know that the time which goes by can never be recaptured and that they, there-fore, need to make the best use they can of this precious resource.

- Making the right choices in life. We need to find out what God wants us to do and then, with His help, set for ourselves realistically achievable goals and work towards these. The expectation and inspiration that the process of goal setting can bring can be very motivating. Setting achievable goals also helps us to chip away at the impossible until it becomes something we can handle, and it gives room for us to be able to express ourselves creatively (instead of being just lazy bystanders in life). Reaching goals is also very motivating, because it shows us that we are fruitful and successful in a measurable way – we do make a difference, and our life does count for something.

- Wanting to improve ourselves, even in areas in which we excel. Seeing ourselves get better at doing something will reinforce our motivation to keep going. The motivation that comes from trying to break records and be successful is also great. This helps us to overcome obstacles and adversity, and to achieve great things in every conceivable area of human endeavour. To place imaginary limitations on ourselves is going to limit our performance, because in the long run these become real limitations. This is because our mind has convinced our body and our will that it cannot be done. As Christians, we need to remember that nothing is impossible to God and that we can do all things through Him who gives us strength (Philippians 4:13). If it is God's will, then it can be done, even by us! We simply need to go to Him in prayer and find out how to do it.

- Considering the consequences of inaction. We can only really do this if we plan and set practical goals for our life and ministry. Once we have done this, we can ask ourselves what the result (or consequence) will be if we fail to achieve them. Will we have depression, financial loss, frustration, loss of motivation etc.? Is it worth it?

- Scheduling the most important tasks to those times when our body and mind are functioning at their peak. If you do not know when these times are, you can do a daily assessment for a month or two to find out. At the end of each day, assess when you did your most (and least) productive work. Was it during the morning, after a stimulating conversation, after a nap, after lunch etc. This personal assessment should be done regularly, and if done, will help us to stay self-motivated throughout life.

Getting into shape

'For physical training is of some value, but godliness has value for all things, holding promise for both the present life and the life to come.'   (1 Timothy 4:8)

This verse is often used as an excuse for avoiding physical exercise, but the truth is that Paul said physical exercise does have some value. The Bible often mentions the need for us to look after our body because it is the temple of the Holy Spirit (1 Corinthians 3:16; 6:15–20; 2 Corinthians 6:16–7:1). If our lack of physical fitness is hampering our service for the Lord, then we need to do something about it!

Exercises

1. Would you classify yourself as a willing, motivated person? In what areas are you motivated? Why these areas? Are they the areas in which God wants you to be motivated? What can/should you do about your motivation to serve the Lord?

2. The difference between a successful person and one who fails or is average, is only slight. What sort of person are you? Can you do anything to improve yourself?

3. Do you enjoy the approval of God in what you are doing? Are you always struggling to do God's will or do you relish tackling the tasks that your calling brings? Have you the assurance and the confidence in yourself and God that enables you to serve without striving?

4. Are you, or those you lead, experiencing commitment problems? What has captivated your heart and theirs? Is this what God wants? How could you encourage commitment? Remember, commitment cannot be forced!

5. It took Thomas Edison over 700 attempts before he succeeded to make a viable light-bulb. How many set-backs does it take for you to give up? If at first you don't succeed, try and try again! Is this true in your life?

6. In our fast-paced world with its instant solutions, perseverance can be thought off as old-fashioned. As a Christian leader should you persevere? Do you? Have you ever achieved anything of note over the years? If not, why not? Is there anything you can/should do about this?

7. If we refuse to take on any challenge, we will never achieve anything! Do you ever take on challenging tasks? How successful are you as a leader? Should you be more successful? What can you do to improve?

8. Is your physical state hindering or helping your work for God? Does looking after your body take up too much of your time and money? Is your shape as God-glorifying as it could/should be?

Chapter 2

Godly Motivation

> *God is just as concerned with why we do His work as He is with the work getting done.*

Introduction

God does want us, as Christians, to be motivated in our service for Him, because He wants His will to be obeyed and His work completed. If motivation enables us to get the job done, the question then arises, 'Does God care what motivates us, as long as the work gets done?' The answer of course is 'Yes'.

In this chapter, we will be looking at the need periodically to examine ourselves prayerfully, so that we can assess where we are heading and what is driving us there. We will also look at a few of the key sources of motivation that God has provided for us as His servants in order to help us carry out His work. And finally, we will look at the positive effect the right people can have on us as we seek to serve the Lord.

The need to examine ourselves periodically

Self-examination should not become a life-style, nor an end in itself for the Christian. This is because, when it is practised too often, it tends to cause people to become too introspective. When this happens, people take their eyes off the Lord and focus instead on their problems and difficulties. We are to seek first the Kingdom of God and His righteousness, and to have God and His will as our life's priority. People who continually look into themselves tend to have selfish, self-centred life priorities, simply because they devote most of their time to trying to find out who they are, why they do what they do, or wallowing in self-pity etc. In fact, looking into ourselves too often can be very dangerous and lead us into great fear, bondage and inaction; especially, if we do nothing but worry about what we discover.

However, there is a place for healthy self-examination (as we have seen in an earlier chapter). This always looks forward with hope to what could be and only behind so that it can learn from any mistakes made. It also helps us to know who we are and what motivates us to do what we do. God does care about why we serve Him. He does care when we are motivated by the wrong things. He wants us to prayerfully consider ourselves, at times, so that we can know how well our walk with Him is going; and so that we can discover what is really going on inside of us. The difference between this, and what we have just warned against, is that God is in control and not us. We are simply giving Him the time and space to point out the things that are not quite right in our lives. Once He has done this, we should ask for His forgiveness and yield these areas of our life into His hand. Some of the things that God may show us as His leaders during times of prayerful self-examination include:

- what our strengths and weaknesses are.
- whether we have unrealistic expectations of ourselves.
- what God's call on our life is.
- what God expects of us.
- whether we are doing something which God never intended us to do (here it is not right to keep pressing on).

- whether we have a persecution complex, which causes us to read threats to ourselves into many situations (whether they are there or not).

- whether we are insecure in our leadership, because we are afraid of people or because we feel we are not competent enough.

- whether we need further training, because of a lack of a skill in a certain important area necessary to our effective functioning as a leader.

- whether we are jealous of someone else.

- whether we are dissatisfied with our position and we want someone else's.

- whether we hold a grudge against someone who has hurt us (which we now need to let go of and allow ourselves to forgive and trust).

An unwillingness to examine ourselves prayerfully tends to make our spiritual growth very difficult, if not impossible; and our ministry effectiveness tends to remain static. We need self-awareness to evaluate our ministry and to get our goals and priorities right in God. The Holy Spirit has been given to be our Counsellor to guide us into all truth (John 14:26: 16:13, 14). He can show us where we need to change and He can help us to change. We simply need to give God room in our lives. We also need to think of ourselves with sober judgement (Romans 12:3), and examine and judge ourselves so that we do not come under the judgement of God (1 Corinthians 11:27–32; 2 Corinthians 10:12, 13; 13:5, 6).

All Christians need to change their thinking to see both themselves, and their work, as God sees them. We do need to be sober in our thinking, but we also need to be willing for God to enlarge our capacity so that we can do more for Him. He has promised to do this, if we faithfully carry out the little things He asks us to do for Him (Luke 19:11–27). This means that we need to keep right with God and make sure we are motivated by the right things. It is true that sometimes God allows His work to be carried out in the most unusual of ways and for the strangest of motives; but, as far as we are concerned, we should be building carefully, because we can only have lasting reward, if we build on the right foundations and with the right materials (1 Corinthians 3:10–15).

It is hard to enter into self-examination when things are bad, but we need to in order to get both ourselves, and our situation, sorted out. We also need to examine ourselves when we fail, because often failure can be remedied. We even need to assess ourselves when things are good, so that we can learn why it worked and do it even better next time. Remember though, our self-worth should not be based on our achievements, our acceptability to other people, or even on our friendships; it should only be based on what God thinks of us.

Some leaders have a great deal of difficulty assessing themselves (most of us are a little paranoid!). It is therefore helpful, at times, for all of us to ask people we trust what they think of us. This question can be asked generally about all of our life or applied to specific areas. It is often true that other people can see us better than we can ourselves. They have not got all the hurts, pride and insecurities (and the internal barriers we have put around these things to protect ourselves from them and the hurt they cause us), that we have inside ourselves which tend to colour the way we view ourselves. We, as leaders, often have to cut ourselves off, to some extent, from self-consciousness to enable us to minister more effectively to other people. This also can cloud our view of ourselves. The best people to go to are people who know us well, like our wives, or friends who are trustworthy and who know how to hear from God. Leaders can also help each other in this area. One way to do this, is to take key church members aside for a retreat (for two or more days, if possible), and look at each other's lives and ministry effectiveness. The pastor, vicar or senior leader will usually have to get things going by modelling the open sharing necessary.

God's great motivators

A demotivated Christian leader is not only possible, it is common! As God's leaders, we need to be God-motivated people, and make sure that we have the right sources of motivation for serving Him. Too many Christian leaders are either too worldly, compromising or vague in their attitude and, therefore, their motivation to serve the Lord is poor. God wants us as His leaders to model the right type of motivation to those we lead and so be good examples to them. He also wants us to be careful, because we can be motivated by negative forces which will eventually destroy us. We will be looking at wrong motivations and the things that demotivate us in the next chapter.

God is concerned about our motives. The end does not justify the means in God's economy. According to God's Word, He understands our motives (1 Chronicles 28:9); He weighs our motives (Proverbs 16:2); He will expose, judge and test our motives (1 Corinthians 4:5; 1 Thessalonians 2:4); and He will not answer our prayers if they are prayed with the wrong motivation (James 4:3). Of course, God is not a 'big brother' figure who is watching over us with a big stick waiting to belt us with it every time we get it wrong. God does love us and He wants only the best for us, but He knows that some things which motivate us can be very damaging to us. He would rather us be motivated by the tools He has provided, and so bring glory to Him and bring our eternal best. The following are some of God's most important sources of motivation to enable effective, fruitful Christian service.

1. The love of God

God's love is unconditional, sacrificial and selfless. It is the Greek word 'agape'. This type of love seeks the welfare of all and the harm of none, as Jesus showed was possible when He came into the world to suffer and die for all mankind. It seeks to bless and to give; and it only wants the best for all to whom it is directed.

> 'Agape expresses the deep and constant love and interest of a perfect being towards entirely unworthy objects, producing and fostering a reverential love in them towards the Giver, and a practical love towards those

who are partakers of the same, and a desire to help others
seek the Giver.'   (W.E. Vine)

The unlimited depth of God's love was revealed to
mankind in His Son Jesus. We can trust and rely on the
love God has for us. Nothing will separate us from this love
(Romans 8:38, 39); and, if we reciprocate it, God will in all
things work for our good (Romans 8:28). Once a person
establishes a personal relationship with the Lord through
faith, 'agape' love can exist, and that love will grow because
of the transforming work of the Holy Spirit within us
(Romans 5:5).

God can only release us to be His undershepherds, when
we can truly say we love Him first, above our secular work
and above ourselves (John 21:15–17). There is no doubt from
Scripture that God loves us dearly (John 3:16; Romans 5:8;
Ephesians 2:4, 5; 5:1, 2), and God commands us to love Him
and other people, and show it by our deeds (Matthew 6:1–4;
Luke 10:27, 28; John 13:34, 35; Romans 12:9, 10; 13:8–10;
1 Corinthians 16:14; Galatians 5:6, 13, 4; 1 Thessalonians
4:9, 10; 2 Thessalonians 3:5; 2 Timothy 2:22–26; 1 Peter
1:22; 4:8; 1 John 3:14–18; 4:7–21). In fact, as Christians, we
are to live a life of love, especially within the community of
believers. It is in the context of this loving family of God that
believers are to grow in their experience of God's love and
reach Christian maturity (Ephesians 3:17–19). Love also
establishes relationships and maintains unity in the body of
Christ (Philippians 2:1–4; Colossians 2:2, 3). Love is the
opposite of selfishness. In fact, those who love are only
fulfilled when they bless those to whom their love is directed.
Selfishness, on the other hand, is never fulfilled – it always
wants more.

As Christians, love should be the chief source of motivation for all that we do (1 Corinthians 13:1–13; 2 Corinthians
5:14). Ministering using the gifts of the Holy Spirit, giving
all we have to the poor, having faith sufficient to move
mountains, and even martyrdom are all tremendous
concepts which every Christian would like to do (to some
extent!), but they are nothing compared with the love of God

according to the Scriptures. In fact, these things are nothing, unless they are done out of a motivation of love. Therefore, if we base our whole life and ministry on these things, we will have done nothing that will be of eternal value to us, unless we had as the driving force behind our actions, the love of God. Love is the most important aspect of Christianity, not healing, prophecy or even evangelism. All our service for God and all the gifts of the Holy Spirit are only meant to be expressions of God's love. Too often we concentrate our attention on the gifts and not the Giver (we forget why the gifts were given in the first place, i.e. to point people to God and to reveal to them the love of God); or we concentrate on our service, and we fail to remember why we are serving.

God's love needs to be at the very centre of our lives and be the motivation for everything we do. The more this is true in our lives, the more it will encourage our commitment to God, prompt our obedience to Him, and enable our labour for Him (John 14:21–24; 1 Thessalonians 1:3; 1 John 5:3). It will also enable us to break free from our self-centred motivational drives, and live instead for God and other people. If Christians did love God with all their heart, strength, mind and soul, there would be no need for any other motivation to serve and obey God (Matthew 22:37–39). As it is, the other motivation sources do help until we reach the perfection for which we should all be aiming.

Seven ways to receive God's love

- Directly from God, i.e. letting God build it into our lives (1 Thessalonians 3:12; 2 Peter 1:3).

- By knowing God in increasing measure. We do this by praying, seeking God and worshipping Him, etc. (John 17:26; 1 John 4:8). God is love; and so spending time in His presence allows us to partake of His love and, therefore, have some of it built into our lives.

- By understanding God's commands and then obeying them (John 14:21). As we put God first in everything we do, it creates a framework for God to work His love into our lives. Not obeying God when He asks us to do something for Him is putting ourselves and our desires above God in that area, i.e. it is, in effect, making ourselves lord of that area. God is then unable to build His love into this part of our life. God only goes where He is wanted and where He is invited to be Lord.

- By yielding our lives into the Holy Spirit's control so that He can pour His love into our hearts and produce in us the fruit of love (Romans 5:5; Galatians 5:22).

- By making a conscious choice to actually put on love and put aside everything that is not of God. The love of God is freely available to us; we can either put it on or reject it, work towards it or ignore it (Colossians 3:12–14). 2 Peter 1:5–9 explains that there is a series of stepping stones which finish in love. We are asked to add these to our lives in increasing measure in order to be effective and productive for God.

- By having a pure heart, a good conscience and a sincere faith (1 Timothy 1:3–7). This passage teaches that Paul's ultimate aim was love. He saw that love wanted to express commitment. Therefore, all the things that need to be done, will be done, in a church in which the people have love as their ultimate aim and their chief source of motivation. Love is the most important thing in God's Kingdom. It is the cement that binds the church together and the church to God.

- By spurring one another on towards love and good deeds (Hebrews 10:24).

'I pray that out of his glorious riches he may strengthen you with power through his Spirit in your inner being, so that Christ may dwell in your hearts through faith. And I pray that you, being rooted and established in love, may have power, together with all the saints, to grasp how wide and long and high and deep is the love of Christ, and to know this love that surpasses knowledge – that you may be filled to the measure of all the fullness of God.'

(Ephesians 3:16–19)

2. The fear of God

The fear of God should be a controlling motive in the life of a Christian. This reverential awe or fear of God influences us to choose to go His way and do His will, instead of doing what we would selfishly choose to do (Psalm 36:1–4; Romans 3:10–18; 2 Corinthians 6:14–7:1 NKJV). The fear of God is described as the beginning of wisdom and knowledge (Psalm 111:10; Proverbs 1:7; 1 Peter 1:17), because it enables us to have a healthy respect for God and shun evil, desiring instead to live obedient godly lives which please our loving heavenly Father. It also helps us to keep our lives in the right perspective, with our will always subservient to the will of the Almighty Creator of all. Taking God into account in this way is the best foundation we can build in order to live disciplined, obedient, righteous, holy lives and to reject anything which may compete with this (Deuteronomy 6:13–19; 10:12–22). In fact, the Lord promises to bless those who fear Him (Psalm 128:1–4).

The fear of the Lord releases us from most of the normal fears which plague mankind and that keep us in bondage or slavery, e.g. the fear of death (Hebrews 2:14, 15); fear of others and what they can do to us (Matthew 10:28; Luke 12:4, 5; Hebrews 13:6; 1 Peter 3:13–16); fear of the enemy (Deuteronomy 20:3, 4); fear of bad news; fear of the unknown; and anxiety, which is the undefinable feeling that something is going to go wrong (Psalm 112:7, 8). This is because we know that no matter what is happening to us or around us, God is for us and He is in control. In fact, God has promised never to leave us or forsake us (Hebrews 13:5); and He has promised that nothing will separate us from His love (Romans 8:38, 39). When we are truly aware of God's power and His loving concern about even the details of our life (Matthew 10:29–31; Luke 12:6, 7), we are released from those lesser fears which may tempt us to compromise or disobey God.

The fear and love of God work together, i.e. we only need to fear God when we step out of His will and, therefore, out of His love. The fear of God can then be a tremendous source of motivation, encouraging us to get back into God's will and, therefore, into His love. Remember, God does not remove His love, we are just stepping out of it in some area if we step into sin. The fear of God can be looked upon as a barrier outside of which are the things which are not of God and inside of which is God's love. Inside there can be no fear, because perfect love drives out all fear (1 John 4:18). When we love and fear God, we need not fear His judgement or punishment, because we will stay right with Him. In fact, we do not even need to fear coming personally and confidently to Him, because of our position in Jesus (Ephesians 3:10–12; Hebrews 10:19–22; Psalm 103:17). As Christians, we have not received a spirit that makes a slave again to fear, but we received the Spirit of sonship that enables us to love God and can call Him our Father (Romans 8:15).

> *'For God has not given us a spirit of fear, but of power and of love and a sound mind.'*   (2 Timothy 1:7 NKJV)

Living in the fear of the Lord was the normal practice for early church members (Acts 9:31). God even acted to encourage His people to hold Him in reverent awe as can be seen by the account of Ananias and Sapphira (Acts 5:1–11). The fear of God helps us to submit to one another, because we realise that we are not competitors as fellow believers, but rather we are serving the same Lord (Ephesians 5:21 NKJV). Remember, God would prefer us to be motivated in our service for Him by love and not by fear of any punishment He may mete out to us. Nevertheless, the Scriptures urge us not to take God lightly, but to serve Him acceptably with reverence and godly fear, for our God is a consuming fire (Hebrews 12:28, 29 NKJV).

> *'Therefore, my dear friends, as you have always obeyed – not only in my presence, but now much more in my absence – continue to work out your salvation with fear and trembling, for it is God who works in you to will and to act according to his good purpose.'*   (Philippians 2:12, 13)

> *'Since you call on a Father who judges each man's work impartially, live your lives as strangers here in reverent fear.'*
> (1 Peter 1:17)

3. Vision from God

This has changed the lives of most of the Bible's major characters, e.g. Abraham, Moses, Samuel, Paul, etc. It can be seen, heard, experienced, personal or prophetically given by God to us; and it is one of the most powerful motivating forces in God's Kingdom. Vision is quickening, because it gets us moving into effective service for God; and it is constraining, because it sets up the boundaries within which we should operate in order to stay in God's will. In fact, Proverbs 29:18 says that without vision people will perish (AV), cast off restraint (NIV), or run wild (Living Bible). We will study this important source of godly motivation in a later chapter.

4. The peace of God

Peace is defined in the dictionary as 'freedom from war or civil disorder; quiet, tranquillity; mental calm; in a state of friendliness; or not at strife'. The peace of God is more difficult to define or understand. In fact, the Word of God says that it transcends all understanding (Philippians 4:7).

The Hebrew word for peace is 'shalom' (salom); and it communicates the meaning of wholeness, completeness, rest, order, harmony/unity and even health, contentment, prosperity and fulfilment, as well as the more usual meaning of absence of strife. It was (and is) used as a blessing and a wish for the recipient's welfare; but more importantly, it speaks of the inner and outer blessing and harmony that comes to a person or people when they live in a close relationship with God and His will. In fact, the peace of God is part of the very nature of God (Judges 6:24; Romans 15:33; 1 Corinthians 14:33; 1 Thessalonians 5:23, 24; Hebrews 13:20) and He alone is the source of real human peace. The Greek word for peace 'eirene', traditionally referred to the orderly prosperous way of life possible in the absence of war. However, New Testament writers modified its meaning to be more like the Hebrew word for peace, 'shalom'. The New Testament also links peace directly to Jesus. After all, He alone is humanity's way to the God of peace.

The peace of God should be clearly evident in the life of believers and outflow in quality relationships between members of the body of Christ, the church. In fact, the peace of God should guard our hearts and minds in Christ Jesus (Philippians 4:7). If you have it, it keeps you going; and if you lose it, you want it back. It can, therefore, govern us (Isaiah 60:17) and be a very useful tool to motivate us to stay right with God. The peace of God should always rule in our heart since as members of one body we were called to peace (Colossians 3:15). This should be true no matter what is happening to us or around us. The Word of God also tells us that the peace of God can give us a future, because there is a future for the man of peace (Psalm 37:37); it brings life to the body, because a heart at peace brings life to the body (Proverbs 14:30); it brings joy (Proverbs 12:20), beauty (Isaiah 52:7) and a harvest of righteousness (James 3:18); and proclaiming or sharing the peace we have been given by God, brings us a greater measure of peace due to the principle of sowing and reaping (Luke 6:38; 2 Corinthians 9:6).

There are a number of ways that we can lose our peace, including:

- unrepented sin (Isaiah 48:22).
- disobedience to God.
- not allowing the peace of God to rule in our hearts, because we are told to 'let' it rule (Colossians 3:15).
- a disorganised inner spiritual life.
- living an unjust life (Isaiah 59:8).

There are also a number of ways to establish the peace of God in our heart. For the Christian, all of these revolve around availing ourselves of the finished work of Jesus at Calvary; and knowing the forgiveness, salvation and peace with God available through repentance from sin and accepting Jesus as our Lord and Saviour (Isaiah 53:5; Romans 5:1; Ephesians 2:14–18). Other ways to keep the peace of Christ firmly ruling in our hearts are:

- Giving the Holy Spirit room in our lives to produce peace, which is one of the fruits of the Holy Spirit (Galatians 5:22).

- By letting the peace of Christ rule in our hearts (Colossians 3:15). This involves setting our will to do the will God.

- As we have seen, God is peace by nature; and so if we spend time with Him and His Word, some of His peace will 'rub off' on us.

- Philippians 4:4–9 gives us a number of things that we can do to establish the peace of God in our hearts. These are: rejoicing in the Lord (vs. 4); letting our gentleness be evident to all (vs. 5); not being anxious about anything, but in everything by prayer and petition with thanksgiving present our requests to God (vs. 6); thinking about what is true, noble, right, pure, lovely, admirable, excellent or praiseworthy, because we become what we input (vs. 8); and putting into practice what we have learned from God and godly men (vs. 9).

- By seeking and pursuing peace (Psalm 34:14; Romans 14:19).

- By loving God's law, because great peace have those who love God's law (Psalm 119:165).

- By finding wisdom, because all her paths are peace (Proverbs 3:13,17).

- By disciplining our children (Proverbs 29:17).

- By keeping our minds steadfast, because we trust in God (Isaiah 26:3; Romans 15:13).

- By pursuing righteousness, because the fruit of righteousness is peace (Isaiah 32:17; Isaiah 57:2).

- By paying attention to God's commands (Isaiah 48:18).

- By being a son of God who is taught by the Lord (Isaiah 54:13).

- By doing good, because glory, honour and peace are given by God to those who do good (Romans 2:10). This explains why many who do not know God seem to be enjoying a life of peace, i.e. they do good to other people and, therefore, they reap the benefit of this promise from God. In Christ, however, we have available to us a far greater depth of peace, because it includes peace with God which all humanity was created to know and, without which, it is impossible to know a real depth of peace.

- By having a mind controlled by the Spirit, because this is life and peace (Romans 8:6).

- By trusting in the God of hope, because then we will be filled with peace (Romans 15:13).

'And the peace of God which transcends all understanding, will guard your hearts and your minds in Christ Jesus.'

(Philippians 4:7)

5. A good conscience

The reason we have included this subject in this section is that we cannot serve the Lord wholeheartedly without having a clear conscience. The Greek word for conscience is 'suneidesis' which literally means 'a knowing with', i.e. knowledge within oneself. The Oxford English Dictionary defines it as 'the internal recognition of the moral quality of one's motives and actions; the faculty or principle which pronounces upon the moral quality of one's actions or motives, approving the right and condemning the wrong'. Our conscience bears witness to our behaviour and either accuses or excuses us (Romans 2:15). Our conscience is not reasonable, it just prompts what it knows is right. We cannot appease it, buy it off or deny it, without building a tremendous tension into our lives. It may be possible to bury this tension for a time, but eventually it will surface, often as an illness or in bitterness. God has given everyone a conscience as an important tool to aid our obedience to and service for Him (Romans 9:1; 13:5; 2 Corinthians 1:12; 5:11; Hebrews 13:18; 1 Peter 3:16–22).

In the ideal situation, our conscience would be programmed always to show us when we are doing (or even thinking of doing) something contrary to the will of God for our lives. Unfortunately, the fall of man into sin has added many extra or different things into our inner man and, therefore, our conscience is not always programmed in the way God ideally wants it to be (Titus 1:15, 16). Conscience alone has never succeeded in producing a truly moral person. As Christians, God needs to do a work in us to renew our minds and thereby retrain or reprogramme our conscience so that it again is activated only by the stimuli that God intended. This takes time; and involves us reading God's Word, obeying His will and yielding our minds to the Holy Spirit, until we begin to react and think in the way God wants us to. Until we reach this place of perfection, we cannot fully trust our conscience. As the apostle Paul said,

> *'I care very little if I am judged by you or by any human court; indeed, I do not even judge myself. My conscience is clear, but that does not make me innocent. It is the Lord who judges me. Therefore judge nothing before the appointed time; wait until the Lord comes. He will bring to light what is hidden in darkness and will expose the motives of men's hearts. At that time each will receive his praise from God.'*
>
> (1 Corinthians 4:3–5)

Believers with a weak conscience have not matured sufficiently to distinguish clearly between what is truly good or godly and what is evil or ungodly, nor to discern what is morally indifferent. These people often manifest a 'legalistic mentality', because they need rules to live by in order to stop them doing the wrong thing. They often put up boundaries that are not particularly of God, but which are, nevertheless, restraints that help them. Their consciences are programmed to keep them within these boundaries. Paul warns us not to cross even these self-imposed boundaries (and so step on our conscience), especially due to pressure from other people. To do so would be not to act from faith, which is sin (Romans 14:1–23, especially vs. 23; Hebrews 11:6).

People with a strong conscience which is based on God's Word, do not need legalistic restraints as much. They have God's boundaries in their heart and this enables them to live the way God wants them to. The strong, however, should not cause their brothers to stumble by what they do (1 Corinthians 8:7–13; 10:23–11:1). Where the will of God is not clear, each person must act in accordance with their own conscience and be careful not to influence others against their convictions. Each individual in this case must be free to respond as they believe God would desire them to. However, when the Word of God is clear on a subject, we must obey it, whatever our conscience is saying.

Remember, although gifts and sacrifice were unable to cleanse from sin, the blood of Christ is sufficient to cleanse us from all sin (Hebrews 9:9–14; 10:19–22). Therefore, when we ask God to forgive us for our sin or for stepping on our conscience, we should expect to be totally free from guilt. Our consciences should be clear, if we have truly repented. Any guilt remaining is usually sourced in the enemy and, therefore, can be resisted and rebuked, because such condemnation is not from God (Romans 8:1, 2).

We should look to see if our conscience is pointing anything out to us. God often uses our conscience to point out something that we need to bring to Him. If we ignore our conscience, we do so at our own peril, because tension will be built into our lives and our conscience will be numbed or dulled and so less of a safeguard for us (1 Timothy 1:19; 4:2). Our motivation to serve the Lord will also suffer, because we will know a nagging sense inside of us that something is wrong. We need a totally clear conscience before we will be able to fully receive and accept God's love into our lives and character (1 Timothy 1:5). Like the apostle Paul, we should always strive to keep our consciences clear before God and man (Acts 24:16).

Friends who motivate us

Every leader needs friends in order to get him through the difficulties that will inevitably face him. These friendships need to be worked at and cultivated by having time invested in them, even time we had set aside for other seemingly important activities. To neglect them can lead to one of the greatest problems of leadership, namely loneliness (or isolation). Friendship is a vehicle by which we can receive life and motivation, and through which we can supply life and motivation to others. Friends can also be exhausting, at times, but the cost is generally worth it. They affirm and encourage us; they are willing to point out our weaknesses and bring the right discipline at the right time; they rejoice when we succeed, and weep when we fall; and they do not envy when we win, or gloat when we fail. Friends support us and stand with us even in our most difficult times. What would we do without them. The tragedy is that many Christian leaders have many acquaintances, but few, if any, real friends.

Gordon MacDonald introduced us to the concept of the different types of friends we all need as leaders in the church in his book *Restoring Your Spiritual Passion*. The following sections are inspired by this material. There are nine types of friends we will consider that all of us need to have, or be to other people, at least at some point in our lives. These are:

1. The discipler

These are friends who give us recognition and who pour into our lives strength, inspiration, passion and vision, enabling us to serve the Lord more effectively. They are available when we need them for courage, approval, guidance and assurance, and they help us to establish and develop our potential in God. Sometimes, they even launch our ministry. They shape our lives and ignite our motivation to serve the Lord. These disciplers are not necessarily our close friends. They tend to come into our lives for a time and for a specific purpose; and they nearly always only make positive contributions to our lives. Unfortunately, we cannot live in the protective shadow of these friends all of the time. We need to learn how to stand on our own two feet and to mature into our own calling in God. Our disciplers simply give us a helping hand along the way. They are the kind of people we can imitate, because of their maturity in God. Biblical examples of this type of friendship would include: Jesus and His disciples; Barnabas and Paul; and Paul and Timothy.

2. The encourager

These friends take note of what we are doing and what we are becoming, and attach value to it, i.e. they let us know we are getting somewhere in God. This encouragement or affirmation is not a vague compliment or an impulsive statement and it certainly is not something for which the person requires reciprocation; but rather it is one person's recognition and positive evaluation of the life and call of God in another person. Without this type of friend, we may never be sure if what we are and what we are doing is actually good enough in God. Without them, we will always be wondering whether we contribute anything meaningful and whether or not we make a difference for God. Satan is always accusing us and seeding negative thoughts into our minds, trying to get us to feel insecure and entertain feelings of being a failure. We need our encouragers to enable us to see things from the right perspective and to keep us on the right road. Without these friends, there would be many more disheartened, demotivated leaders; and also many more leaders who gave up their ministry altogether. People who act as this type of friend must be very careful to encourage or affirm only what is of God in the other person and not just be a 'yes man' to them.

3. The exhorter

These friends tell us the truth, even if it sometimes hurts. They are willing to speak to our faces what other people are probably speaking behind our back. Many people in leadership find these people hard to take, because they are so used to being the person with all the right answers. If we are honest, at times, we need to receive what our rebukers say (and change our lives accordingly), in order to keep ourselves right before God. Obviously, it is not right to modify our behaviour so that we come into line with every negative word that comes our way, but it is right to weigh any words of rebuke we receive to see what they contain. If there is any kernel of truth in the words (and there often is), then we will be a better servant of God, if we accept it and modify our life accordingly. A good practice is to take words of rebuke to God in prayer, and ask Him whether they are true and what we should do with them.

In Christian circles, we are often too nice to each other and we tolerate some of the most appalling behaviour. We tend to live like this, because we confuse love with sloppy sentimentality and, therefore, we are unwilling to hurt each other's feelings or say a negative word about another believer. Positive criticism can be one of the most valuable resources available to us. God wants us to live in reality; and truth spoken in God's way and in God's time, can help us do this and be a life-changing thing. Rebukes are often the most effective moments of learning we can experience. They often set us free from things that before hand were hindering our ministry or quenching our motivation to serve the Lord (Proverbs 27:5, 6; Proverbs 28:23). We need to be corrected when we are wrong; we need to be pushed when we are lazy; we need to be envisioned when we become complacent; and we need to be redirected when we are straying from God's path.

When we receive a rebuke, our self-image is threatened. God, however, has not asked us to defend this, but to humble ourselves under His mighty hand that in due time He may exalt or lift us up (1 Peter 5:6). If you feel that the Lord would have you play the role of a rebuker, then remember that all things need to be done with a motivation of love. Only rebuke if it is for the other person's good and it is something that they will be able to do something about. We need to watch out for those who use a rebuke to try and put us down so that they can get one over us or so that they can feel bigger. If love is really our motivation for rebuking, then it follows that it will cost us and hurt us to do it, because when you love someone, you will not want to hurt them (2 Corinthians 2:2–4).

4. The intercessor

These are friends who hold us before the Lord in prayer. They are friends who tend to seek us out and ask us how things are going. We should share intelligently what is on our heart with these people. God can tell them the right things to pray for us, but it is also helpful, when possible, to let them know where we are at with God, what we are doing for God, and what our needs are in God. It is also important to encourage these friends by letting them know how God has provided for us. We should never neglect those who pray for us, because our life in God and our motivation to serve Him depends on prayer. We need those who will pray for us, whatever our level of maturity in God. Those with leadership responsibilities, however, need prayer as a matter of urgency.

5. The partner

These are friends with whom we share our work load and our lives. They are team-mates! They keep us motivated, because they are aiming for the same things we are and they are heading in the same direction that we are heading, at least for a season. They, therefore, encourage us and prod us into action, so that the partnership we form with them will achieve its goals. It is like the carrying of a heavy load that requires everybody to lift in order to get it off the ground. If one person refuses to co-operate, the load will stay where it is. Partners have picked up part of the same load that we are carrying and they have accepted responsibility for it. These people are usually there when we need them and can empathise with us, because when we are hurting because of the work, they often are; and they share our joys and successes. Partnerships are usually synergistic. This means the amount of work that can be achieved by the partners as a team is greater (usually much greater) than that which could be achieved by the partnership members working independently of each other, i.e. the whole is more effective than the sum of the parts. Partnerships enable us to reach our full potential in God, and they give us courage, motivation and strength. Working as part of a team is also very encouraging, especially when the team sees results. If you are married, your most important partner should be your spouse.

6. The shepherd

These are the understanding friends who lead, feed, shield and shepherd us. They come alongside of us and pull us up when we are down; they encourage us when we are weak; they come and help us get back on our feet when our motivation to serve the Lord is suffering; they care for us when we are hurting; and they bring order from confusion. These friends sense where we are at with God and in ourselves, and they approach us and give to us at our point of need. They are trustworthy people to whom we can run when we are at the end of ourselves and know that there we will find the encouragement, help and ministry we need.

7. The servant

These are friends who will willingly do practical things for us. They tend to be friends who are always available whenever we need them. Nothing is too menial or outrageous for these faithful people, because they have enjoined themselves to us to enable the work we do for the Lord. They help our motivation, because they take some of our work load from us and, therefore, give us more time to get on with the things we know should be doing for God. We need to take care to recognise and honour this form of friendship that all too often is taken for granted or goes unnoticed. Not to do so, may cause the person to feel used and for them to lose their motivation to serve us. We must also not be too proud to accept the help these people offer to us. Remember though, not to force people to serve you in this way. Such service is a calling in God which should not be forced.

8. The disciple

These are friends for whom God has made us responsible for a time. It is our job to train and help these are people, who want to receive and learn from us. Although we may be giving much of our time and energy to these friends, we are more than happy to do so, because we see the potential in them for God. Jesus calls us to be His disciples and, at times,

part of this calling is to train other people to work alongside
of us in the Kingdom of God. There is little more stimulating
to our motivation to serve the Lord than seeing men and
women who have been helped or encouraged by what we
have been able to build into their lives. Again, it is must be
remembered that we should never force anyone to become
our disciple.

9. The social friend

These are friends with whom we can relax and have a good
time. Even Christian leaders need to do this from time to
time, because God created us as social beings. These friends
are often people with whom we share common hobbies,
interests or sports. Sharing these activities with these people
helps us to unwind and occasionally get our mind off our
work. All Christians need to do this, and to have a friend to
share it with, makes it more worthwhile and therapeutic.
These are also people we can have a cup of coffee with and
know that we will not get preached at or discuss work unless
we want to. The only thing to watch with this type of
friendship is that we keep it in perspective. We will enjoy
the activities we engage in while carrying out this type of
friendship, but we must not let these activities take up too
much of our time or let them captivate our heart, instead of
the Lord and His work.

It must be noted that the same person may be a different
type of friend to us at various times. We need to cultivate
friendships in God and look for the people to whom
God wants us to be such a friend. It is important, however,
that we do not model our lives blindly on just one or two
people, because this tends to cause us to idolise or hero
worship them. We should only model ourselves on Jesus
and the aspects of His character that we see in other
people.

Many churches will not survive unless the practice of
friendship making improves in them. New church members
want to feel welcome in a church and find an atmosphere
of love in it. Church growth strategists have discovered
that they will then need to have found as many as seven

meaningful relationships in that church before they will commit themselves to it for a long period. As a rule, it is meaningful relationships, and not structures or programmes, that hold people in a church. Loneliness will drive people away and turn them against the church, because they do not expect to be lonely in what is supposed to be a loving, caring environment. People need at least to feel wanted.

Friendships which become cliques are wrong, because other people are excluded from and even feel threatened by such a group. However, friendships established with Jesus as the foundation, last and make a tremendous impact both on our life and on the lives of those to whom we come into contact day by day. The church would be a better place if all leaders had the right friends and all church members worked at this very important aspect of church life. Motivation would increase, more of God's work would be done, and God's love would flow more freely (and this never fails).

Exercises

1. Do you know how you are getting on in God? Are you growing in your relationship with Him or are you just treading water? Do you ever prayerfully examine your walk with God? Should you? What are some of the dangers in doing this? Have you let self-examination become a stifling pre-occupation with yourself? Is self-examination worth the risk?

2. Write down some realistic goals for every area of your life. Pray about this before you do. Then rate the difficulty you are going to have in achieving each of these. If it is too difficult, make the goal easier! Try to separate external expectations (what other people expect of you!), from internal ones (what you expect of yourself!), because this will help you see what or who is motivating you in this area. Finally, examine how closely your sense of worth is wrapped up in your fulfilment of your expectations.

3. If love is shown by the actions it prompts, how much love do you have in your life? Do you need to ask God for more? What is the chief thing that motivates your service for God?

4. How much reverence and awe do you have for God? Do you go to God with the right attitude of heart? How wise are you in the choices you make?

5. What vision has captivated your heart? Is it of God? Are you excited about your work for God? Do you feel like you are perishing or sinking or acting in an unrestrained manner, because you have no direction or guidelines from God; or are you just doing your own thing and hoping for the best?

6. Is the peace of Christ ruling in your heart? If not, why not; and what are you going to do about it?

7. Is your conscience clear before God? Are you feeling guilty about anything? What is the source of this; and should you do anything about it? Does God ever condemn us?

8. There are too many demotivated lone-rangers in the church in positions of leadership. Are you one? What can you do about this situation? Are there any old friends you can look up? Do you need to work at the friendship you have with your wife?

9. Did the apostle Paul have friends? Was he committed to them? Did he continually affirm them and work at these friendships? Why did he do this? Did he depend on his friends? What lessons can we learn from Paul in this area?

Chapter 3

Losing Our Way

> *Demotivation and wrong motivation are not terminal problems for Christian leaders who keep their eyes on the Lord and who seek to live obedient lives which bring glory only to God.*

Introduction

In Christian terms, what are demotivated people like? The answer to this is obviously complex. Human beings are affected by a variety of different stimuli and each of us react differently to these. However, we can generalise and say that demotivated people tend to see life as a meaningless set of actions which hold little joy or scope for personal fulfilment. The types of questions these people ask themselves include:

- Where is all this going?
- Why am I doing this?
- What is the point?
- When will I discover rest and peace again?
- I used to enjoy this, so why isn't it fun any more?
- Why am I so frustrated, depressed and/or tired?
- Why do I feel trapped?

- Why do I feel like giving up and running away?
- Why don't I even like other Christians?
- Where has all my energy and drive gone?
- Why do I like my hobby, sport and/or work, more than my Christianity?
- Where is God anyway?

If we are honest, all of us ask this type of question from time to time. We tend to ask ourselves these questions when we feel we are losing (or we have lost) our way. Our spirits are deflated and life is no longer a challenge. It either becomes a set of days for which we have to steel ourselves in order to get through or we adopt the motto, 'Anything for an easy life!'. We have stopped trying to find the answers or achieve a break through. We have been hurt one too many times and we do not want to be disappointed again. Our hopes are dashed and we dare not hope again. We do what is expected of us and hope that no one will notice that we are down. Often during these times our credibility to other people becomes very important to us and we fear losing face or respect more than just about anything else. This is because our self-image is at an all time low and we need to salvage something by maintaining the respect of our peers or anyone willing to give it to us.

People who live long enough in this state tend to join the ranks of the cynical. They have given up trying to make a difference and they have settled into a routine which enables them to survive and get by. These people often say they have been around long enough to see it all before. They know the difficulties and the reasons why you cannot do certain things. They are often the first ones to pour cold water on any new idea or to point out why it won't work. They have given up! They have lost their freshness and their first love for the Lord, and they have either quenched the fire of the Holy Spirit within them or hardened themselves to His work.

In this chapter, we are going to consider some of the many enemies which try to prevent us from living a motivated

Christian life. All leaders will make mistakes, but some of them, when made too often, can be disastrous to our Christian walk and our service for the Lord. We will also look briefly at some of the ways a Christian leader can avoid these pitfalls and stay motivated in his service for God.

Drive without discernment

It is very easy, even for a Christian leader, to be very highly motivated for the wrong reasons. People motivated in such a way tend to see the need for a job to get done, but they have forgotten that God requires a job to be done in His way and in His time. God wants to be put first in our lives and for us to work for His glory and the extension of His Kingdom. He wants us to be successful and fruitful 30, 60 or 100 times, but not by just any means or at any cost. People who are highly motivated for the wrong reasons have been called 'driven' people, which is a very apt description.

Driven people tend to substitute power and success for their need for love and acceptance. They have often been brought up in a family where striving for predominance or success was a way of life and the only way acceptance was achieved (whereas failure was punished). Many driven people are trying to make up for past mistakes or are attempting to cover up a shameful background. These people often see everything in terms of winning and losing; and they need to win, because this to them is the evidence of their self-worth and the proof that they are valuable, important and right in what they are doing. Some questions you could ask yourself to see if you are such a person include:

- Do you only feel good when you have accomplished something?
- Is goal achievement more important to you than personal integrity or morality?
- Do you ever lie to yourself about your motives?
- Do you care what other people think about you, or are your relationships with other people selfishly motivated,

i.e. do you group other people into 'unimportant' and 'those who can help you succeed' categories?

- Are your goals more important to you than other people?

- Do you leave behind you a trail of worn-out, disillusioned, spiritually bankrupt people?

- Do you boast to others about how much you do?

- Do you strive to make yourself indispensable to the action?'

- Do you see life only in terms of results?

- Does it matter how you achieve the results?

- Are you very concerned about the size of your office, your job title, the type of car you drive, or any other symbols of success?

- Are you always wanting to be involved in something that is getting bigger and better, and to have an increasingly important position in this?

- Are you never satisfied with yourself, your position or other people?

- Do you react with anger when other people let you down, oppose you, are disloyal, disagree with, or criticise you?

- Are you so busy that your family relationships, friendships and your walk with God suffer badly?

- Would you know what to do with yourself if your job was suddenly taken away from you?

- What gives you your sense of self-worth?

Many Christians put up with much from driven people, because they mistakenly believe that you cannot argue with success, or they are afraid to oppose them (even those who are in a position to do so!). Unfortunately, many church leaders fit into this category of person, because these people tend to be high achievers and, therefore, make it to the top in any field in which they choose to work.

If you realise you are such a person, there is hope. The first step to being released from your bondage (for indeed, this is what it is!), is to assess your motives and values realistically, with God's help. You may need the help of other Christians whom you respect in order to do this, because they can sometimes see things in you that you refuse to see in yourself. You need to meet with God over a period of time and ask Him to help you discover the root cause of your problem and the way in which it is expressed in your life. You then need to admit to yourself that you are motivated by the wrong things. It is important that you take this to the Lord and ask for His forgiveness, especially if you have neglected your relationship with Him or you have hurt other people. You may also need to go to the people you have hurt and ask for their forgiveness. Finally, you need to ask God to show you what He has called you to do for Him and how to fulfil that call in His way and in His time. As you begin to do this, you will find that the peace and rest of God will return to you, and you will start enjoying your work and your relationships with other people. Remember, it is alright to work hard for God, but we need to do this in His way.

Words without power

> *'For the kingdom of God is not a matter of talk but of power.'*
> (1 Corinthians 4:20)

There are two Greek words for 'power' in the Scriptures. The first is 'dunamis' which speaks of ability or might, and it refers to the power of God to act, both independently of His servants and through His servants. The verse quoted above uses this word. The second is 'exousia' which speaks of privilege and authority, and it refers to the freedom or right of God or His servants to act. The distinction between the two words can be seen in the contrast between a ten-ton truck going 70 mph (dunamis) and a traffic police-man directing traffic (exousia). Both speak of different dimensions of the idea of power. Christians are called by God to live in both of these dimensions of the concept of power.

Christians, like all people in the world, have at their disposal the power of words. These can encourage, upbuild, edify, save, teach, heal, or praise; or they can pull down, harm, hurt, condemn, enrage, manipulate, or destroy (James 3:1–12). Words are very powerful things. As God's children, we have been given an extra responsibility in that we are Christ's ambassadors to the world, and even to the rulers and authorities in the heavenly realms (Ephesians 3:10, 11). We, therefore, need to keep a reign on our tongue and use this powerful tool only as an instrument which glorifies God (James 1:26).

However, it is all too common for Christians to utter words without power. This is what the verse quoted at the beginning of this section was referring to. A Christian should live a life in which the 'dunamis' of God is coupled with the 'exousia' of God, i.e. the power of God to change things should accompany the authority given by God to change things. As Christians, the authority comes as we understand God's will for us through reading His Word or by hearing Him speak to us directly in some way. This 'quickened' word from God will then create faith in us. As we step out in that faith, the power of God will be released to achieve His will (Romans 10:17; Mark 11:22–24). Nothing is impossible to those who act on God's behalf in this way. It enables us to experience what Jesus did during His earthly ministry (John 14:12). Methodology, formulas and packages will crush people, if we try and substitute them for the real power of God. Of course, it is taken for granted that before all this is possible, the person has totally submitted their life to God and so is living under His authority.

Many Christians are not effective for God because they speak out words without power. If we preach or testify to others about God and what He has done for humanity, without the power of God affirming (or backing up) what we say, then we can often do more harm than good. People will probably expect to see results, but when none are forth coming, they will tend to switch off and become hardened to the gospel message. Many Christians in the church today verbally ascent to the power of God, but they live lives which deny their words. On the other hand, if when the Kingdom of God is preached, there are signs following (as there should be), people will be convinced of the existence of God and many will turn to Him (Mark 16:15–18; Acts 8:5–8; 13:6–12). Things should happen when the Word of God is proclaimed or testified to and lives should be changed as a result. A 'quickened' word from God will work, when we accompany it with faith.

Our motivation to serve the Lord will decrease if we speak out words that in theory should have an effect in a certain way, but in practice do not. Remember, if you do not seem to have a 'quickened' word from God on which to step out in faith, don't panic! Ask God for one. He has promised that those who ask will receive, those who seek will find, and to those who knock the door will be opened (Luke 11:9, 10).

Listening without doing

> *'Humbly accept the word planted in you, which can save you. Do not merely listen to the word, and so deceive yourselves. Do what it says. Anyone who listens to the word but does not do what it says is like a man who looks at his face in the mirror and, after looking at himself, goes away and immediately forgets what he looks like. But the man who looks intently into the perfect law that gives freedom, and continues to do this, not forgetting what he has heard, but doing it – he will be blessed in what he does.'* (James 1:21–25)

The word of God revealed to us needs to be obeyed and not just listened to. This obedience goes far beyond the more common responses of many Christians, namely emotional excitement or intellectual stimulation, which are often not backed up by any action. In fact, words received on this level tend to be quickly forgotten. Many Christians are waiting for the right feeling before they will obey God, because they find that obedience is easier when they do this. Other Christians are waiting for God to bless them in order to make the cost of obedience easier to bear. Of course, God does want us to weigh the cost (Luke 14:25–35), but He does not want us to stop there. He wants us to mature to a place where we obey Him, no matter how we feel or what the cost. This maturity is only reached step by step as we obey God and do the little things He asks us to do for Him. Then, as we prove faithful in this, God will take us on to a place of greater maturity in Him and ask us to do bigger things for Him. Unless we start to live a life in which we listen to God and do what He says, our motivation to serve the Lord will progressively die. This is because we will not be moving forward in our Christian life, and we will not be as fruitful and effective for God as we know we ought to be.

> *'Therefore everyone who hears these words of mine and puts them into practice is like a wise man who built his house on the rock. The rain came down, the streams rose, and the winds blew and beat against that house; yet it did not fall, because it had its foundation on the rock. But everyone who hears these words of mine and does not put them into practice is like a foolish man who built his house on sand. The rain came down, the streams rose, and the winds blew and beat against that house, and it fell with a crash.'*
>
> (Matthew 7:24–27)

Lives without integrity

> *'Whoever claims to live in him must walk as Jesus did.'*
>
> (1 John 2:6)

To live a life of integrity in the Kingdom of God is to live a righteous, holy life. This is a possibility for the Christian because of the work of Jesus. Every time we do fail, we can simply confess our sin to God, repent of it (i.e. turn our backs and walk away from it), and God has promised to restore us to a place of cleanness in His sight (1 John 1:7–9). If, however, we are harbouring some form of sin in our life and we are unwilling to repent of it, then this will act as a barrier between us and God and we will begin to lose our motivation to serve Him. This will be because God will seem more distant to us and because we are not living in the way He intended us to live. In fact, living with sin in our life is extremely dangerous to our motivation to serve the Lord. We may be able to function well on the outside, but eventually the sin will so eat away at us and get such a strong grip on us, that it will begin to choke the life out of us.

Integrity also involves recognising our true feelings and motives and expressing them honestly. As Christians, we should live lives that are honest both with ourselves and with God (after all, we cannot hide anything from Him anyway!). The opposite of integrity is hypocrisy. Jesus seemed to be very concerned with this (Matthew 6:5, 16; 23:13–36; 24:51). Unfortunately, too much hypocrisy has taken root in the church and it has taken its toll. It has caused people to hide from themselves or to numb themselves to their consciences. Hyprocrisy eventually will destroy a person's self-worth and any godly motivation they may have had.

> *'Above all else, guard your heart, for it is the wellspring of life.'*   (Proverbs 4:23)

Another aspect of lives without integrity is particularly relevant to those leaders who teach. We should never teach anything without at least first starting to live in the good of it. If what we are teaching cannot be seen to be working first in us, then it is going to be very difficult for other people to receive that truth. (Some will of course, as God can use us despite what we do, at times.) This is even more true if we live lives that contradict the truth we are teaching. If, however, the truth that we are teaching about does work for us, then other people will see this and want what we have got. It will give our teaching credibility, and enable many more people to receive, and act on the truth we teach to them.

Many Christian leaders have a pressure on them to 'come up with the goods' when they preach, so they grab a hold of any truth that sounds good and they teach this. This type of approach to teaching may get a good response at the time, but people tend to forget such messages as soon as they hear the next sermon that is communicated well or that takes their fancy. Leaders who do this, tend to find that their congregations do not change and that they themselves are just 'treading water' or staying where they are spiritually.

A loss of motivation will often occur as a result of these things, especially if the leader has the courage to be honest about themselves and their situation.

We need to live lives of integrity as Christians. To lie to ourselves or to try and cheat or do it the easy way, may give us short-term success, but in the long-run, we will find that it does not really work and it may even cost us our motivation to serve the Lord. We need to be careful how we live and be honest with ourselves and with God; and we need to live lives that bring Him glory. We also need to have God's standards for our life and not live as the majority want, because even in a church, their standards may differ from God's. The normal is not necessarily the right. We need to allow God to determine what is right and let Him define what living a life of integrity means.

Gifts without application

> *'Each one should use whatever gift he has received to serve others, faithfully administering God's grace in its various forms.'*   (1 Peter 4:10)

There are many Bible passages which stress our accountability to God for how we steward (or manage on God's behalf) the gifts and talents that He has given to us (e.g. the parable of the talents: Matthew 25:14–30). There are other passages which teach us that we will be held accountable for how we care for those around us (e.g. the parable of the sheep and the goats: Matthew 25:31–46). God gives His servants gifts and talents and material possessions in order to enable them to serve Him. They are not given primarily for our own pleasure or for us to gloat over; and they are certainly not given so that we can gain worldly wealth, position or honour. God wants to be made Lord of all of our lives, and unless we see ourselves as God's servants who only do His will, we will find that we become demotivated in our service for the Lord. This is because we will start to gain our motivation from the wrong things and so alienate ourselves from God and the things He has provided to motivate us in

His service. Remember, any gift we receive from God is not for our own benefit primarily, but to enable the work of the Kingdom of God. We, therefore, need to sharpen and polish these gifts and do the best we can with them for the glory of God.

God also gives gifts to us such as a relevant prophecy or a godly rebuke from a spiritual elder. We need to receive these when we know they are from the Lord, and apply them to our lives with God's help and enabling. Not to do so is to reject God and His word to us.

Another enemy to our motivation in this area is to be given a gift or a vision from the Lord that we are unable to apply for the moment, and to have a wrong reaction to this. This may be caused by people rejecting our ideas for the right or wrong reasons; or because the timing is not right in God; or even because we have got it wrong. Each time a dream is deflated or a gift unable to be used, for whatever reasons, it hurts us, and we can easily become disillusioned. If this happens, our motivation to serve the Lord can suffer quite badly. We need to go to God at such times and throw ourselves on Him. King David did this time and time again, and found his courage and motivation return as He spent time in God's presence. Often, we go through these times, because God wants to test us and to see if we truly believe that what He says will happen. We need to learn to trust God during these times and know that His word will not return to Him empty, but will accomplish the purpose for which He sent it (Isaiah 55:11). If God has spoken, it will happen, even if it does take a little time. Opposition should be expected, but we should never let the enemy have an opportunity to demotivate us by a wrong reaction to this opposition, whatever form it takes. We need to learn how to put our full confidence in God and His Word, and trust Him whatever our circumstances.

Activity without discipline

Too many churches have too many choices of what should fill their members time and, as a result, they have many tired, worn-out people who have no more energy or motivation left to do the things they know God would really prefer them to do. One anointed, fruitful prayer meeting is better than six prayer meetings held because we always have them or because we feel it would be a good idea. Churches need to have a disciplined, wise agenda of programmes for their members and a disciplined choice of the leaders to run them. Someone once said, 'Christianity is a life-style, not a life-sentence!' Christians should be able to enjoy themselves, at times, and be able to spend time with their families. Some churches need to make room in their busy agenda for this to be possible. People will eventually stop coming to our churches unless we do. The frightening thing with this mentality is that it usually affects the willing people in the church and it leaves us instead with demotivated, tired people who often feel they have let us down or failed us. When other church members see this, volunteers tend to become harder to find. Church leaders can often compound this situation by wrongly diagnosing a commitment problem in their church, and so encourage church members to greater commitment. Unfortunately, they only succeed in heaping condemnation on those who were once willing servants, but who have been milked dry and have no more to give (at least until they have had a good rest).

Many churches load down their people with so many tasks that their people are no longer effective in what they do for God. Even the leaders have often spread themselves so thin due to the bulk of what they have taken on, that they cannot do justice to any of their activities. This forces them to do the minimum they can to try keep everybody happy and usually they fail to do this. They are like David in Saul's armour, they can hardly move. Like David, these leaders would be far better off removing the armour (or encumbrances that other people try to force on them), and doing the thing that God has equipped or gifted them to do. David was only able to slay Goliath, because He was getting on with the Lord's work and He stuck with his gift, i.e. the proven weapon that had already killed a lion and a bear. The task of reaching the world is the church's Goliath. We will be far more likely to be successful in our part of that task, if we only take on God's burdens, instead of weighing ourselves down with many burdens of our own or burdens which other people try to put onto us. As Christians, we should only work in areas to which God has called us and for which He has adequately gifted us.

Many Christians want to do all they can for the Lord. They know that they are responsible before God for their lifestyle and that they have a contribution to make to the Kingdom of God. They see their abilities and energies as something they must share with others or with the organisation of which they are a part. However, the more willing they are to get involved (especially if they are talented and successful), the more opportunities and sometimes even demands, seem to come their way. This often results in increasing fatigue, exhaustion, weariness and loss of motivation. Busyness needs to be disciplined, otherwise the tiredness and general loss of motivation that will result will decrease the quality of these people's service for the Lord. They will tend to become more sloppy, unreliable and prone to having conflicts with other people. Eventually a crisis will arise and people in this position will quit. Too many Christians get consumed by over-loading themselves with activities. These activities might be good, challenging, need-oriented things which God seems to have given us the talent to do successfully, but it may not be God's time or His will for us to take them on at that moment. Christians often take on activities because they want to be liked and they fear the rejection that a refusal may bring. Others take on activities because they are ambitious and they want to be seen; or because they do not want to be left out; or even because they did not have the courage to say, 'No'. These should never be the reasons we take on an activity. We need to be in constant touch with our God and we should only be doing the things that He directs us to do.

People in a tired, disillusioned, demotivated state are very prone to enemy attack, because they have often taken their eyes off the Lord and let their Christian discipline slip. These people are then very vulnerable and it can cause them to act in ways which are disastrous to their walk with God, e.g. men having adulterous affairs (in order to try and find comfort, acceptance, or an escape from their loneliness), or church leaders giving up altogether. Fatigue makes cowards of most people, and often causes us to react foolishly and rashly to difficult situations.

Taking our eyes off the Lord at any time is wrong, especially if we focus our attention on our problems and difficulties instead. This tends to cause us to mix up our priorities, i.e. we give more and more of our effort and time to ourselves and our work, and less and less to God and His Word. This will eventually cause us to dry up spiritually and, as a result, cause us to either lose our motivation to serve God or to look for motivation from the wrong sources. The work may get done, but our walk with the Lord will be poor. If we really knew the cost of this type of behaviour in terms of our eternal standing with God, I think it would shock many of us. The Lord does care what motivates us and what drives us to get the job done. Taking their eyes off the Lord can cause leaders, who may have started doing God's work, to end up doing their own thing. This is because these people fail to see the change in direction God had for them. The tragedy is that many of these leaders still believe they are doing God's will. We all need, at times, to take a hard look at ourselves. We need to get before God and allow Him to point out anything that needs to change or anything that needs to get back in line with His will for our lives. We need to keep our eyes fixed on Jesus, the author and perfecter of our faith and, therefore, enable Him to have the opportunity and the room to do whatever is necessary in our lives (Hebrews 12:1–3). God wants to perfect our walk with Him continually and enable us to be increasingly effective for Him. We need to be open to change and never dig ourselves into a rut out of which we refuse to move.

Christians are definitely too busy if their Christian disciplines suffer, e.g. waiting on the Lord, prayer, or reading God's Word, etc. If we are truly doing God's will (with no added extras), God will have built in time for us to spend with Him and His Word. John Wesley once said,

> 'Though I am always in haste, I am never in a hurry because I never undertake more work than I can go through with calmness of spirit.'

This is good advice, especially for Christian leaders. Remember, it is not just running that wins the race. The winner of the prize is usually the one who sets their lifestyle and disciplines their life in order to run in such a way that they will win the prize. These people also make sure that they do not get disqualified along the way (1 Corinthians 9:24–27).

Some Christians get demotivated simply because they fail to win any prizes or they do not seem to meet with success. Such people need to look to the Lord and trust Him – God may be storing up their treasure in heaven (Matthew 6:19–21). They also need to continue to live in a motivated, disciplined fashion, knowing that God can never be out-given and that He will reward them in His time (1 Corinthians 3:10–15). God only brings forth His fruit in season (Psalm 1:1–3). We need to find out from God what season it is for us and work accordingly with all our might, being careful not to be side-tracked by other things that may try and demand our time. As Christians, we only need to be doing the good work God has prepared in advance for us to do (Ephesians 2:10). This is not, however, an excuse to be unprepared at any particular time, because God wants us to be prepared in season and out of season (2 Timothy 4:2), and so be ready to do whatever He asks us to do, whenever He asks us to do it. Our job is to do God's will and to live a life which is so disciplined that our chances for fruitfulness and success for God are maximised.

Issues without judgement

> 'For it is time for judgement to begin with the family of God; and if it begins with us, what will the outcome be for those who do not obey the gospel of God?' (1 Peter 4:17)

Every Christian is going to appear before the judgement seat of Christ. There we are going to receive what is due to us for all the things we have done while on earth, whether good or bad (2 Corinthians 5:10; Romans 2:16). Therefore, we must live our lives as those who must give an account. Leaders have the added responsibility of also being accountable for those they lead and what they teach (Hebrews 13:17; James 3:1). Christians, and especially Christian leaders, need to be very careful how they live. If we hold anything against anyone else, we need to sort it out in God's way (Matthew 18:15–20), because we know that we dare not do anything apart from God's will. We should never speak out negative things about other people, but rather sort them out. Forgiving other people needs to be a normal part of our life. God has forgiven us much and He expects us to forgive others (Mark 11:25). Those speaking in the church should speak as if they are speaking the very words of Christ (1 Peter 4:11), and those who listen to that word should know that they will be held accountable for their response to it, if indeed the word that was spoken was from God (Ezekiel 33:8, 9).

The threat of God's judgement should not be looked upon as a hold that He has on us in order to keep His church in bondage or to enforce obedience. God's judgement should be looked upon with joy by the Christian, because we know that we will receive a reward for all the work we do for God on this earth (Matthew 16:27; Luke 6:35; Ephesians 6:8). Everything we do is noticed by God. In fact, nothing good that we do will be overlooked or forgotten. The judgement of God should hold no fear for those who do what is right in God's sight. The only reasons that Christians fear God's judgement is that they do not know Him well enough or they know that they are not doing the things that He would have them do. The truth is that we have a loving, merciful God who is willing to forgive us for anything, if we repent, turn to Him, confess our sin, and ask for His forgiveness.

Some Christians so fear God's judgement that it causes them great distress. These people tend to have a wrong image of the Fatherhood of God. They need to come to God and His Word, and begin to discover the true character of Him whom they serve and realise just how much He loves them. To fear

God's judgement in a debilitating way is to lack trust in Him and this is to sin. If you have been guilty of this, go to God and ask for His forgiveness.

On the other hand, many Christians are very quickly demotivated in their service for God, because they do not fully believe that a loving God will judge them. Therefore, they tend to live life as they please, instead of doing God's will. They make up the rules for their life (instead of God), and they wonder why, at times, things do not work out according to their plans (often they even blame God when things go wrong). We need to live with our hearts in heaven, and use the knowledge that God will judge us to keep us living righteous, holy and obedient lives which are yielded totally to God. We get our heart in heaven by putting our treasure there (Matthew 6:19–21). Building treasure in heaven by faithfully obeying God's will in His way, will help us to be less concerned about building for ourselves a treasure here on earth. Earthly treasure building seems to be one of the greatest sources of motivation for living selfishly, rather than selflessly as God wants. We need to look to God for our rewards and not to the world or to other people. Besides, earthly treasures have a habit of rusting and being rather meaningless when we die.

Experience without Word

The Word of God should be the central pillar in the church. (Remember, Jesus is described as the Word of God: John 1:1–14). The Word of God needs to be the standard or ruler by which we measure everything we do in the church. Many Christians (indeed, many churches!) live with the Word of God in a secondary place. It is used as a backup or 'proof' for their experiential Christianity or is thought of as a fallible book of great writings. The truth is that the Word of God is the main source of our information of who God is and how He wants us to live. If the Word of God is not central to our life, we are in grave danger. God's Word has been given for our instruction (2 Timothy 3:16, 17). To ignore, deny or change this book of God's words is to deny God Himself. In fact, to neglect the Scriptures in any way is to undermine one of Christianity's chief foundations and leave us on very shaky ground. To do so can leave us forming just another religion (often one we have made up ourselves!) which, in the long run, will not work. Many Christians have been disillusioned or hurt, and some have even embraced incomprehensible heresies, because they have turned away from God's Word. These people have no certainty of what the truth is and so they substitute something else for it. They then have to hope that they are right. In fact, many also couple hard work to their faith in an unconscious attempt to make their beliefs more acceptable to God. Such blind hope has no hope of being realised in the long-term. The only hopes that are certain are those which are based on God's Word.

Labour without love

As we have seen in the previous chapter, God wants love to be the chief source of motivation for all our actions. For this to be possible, we need to allow the love of God to enter our life and to permeate every corner of it. God's love can be relied on, because it never fails and, therefore, we can base our life with confidence on it. Love also covers a multitude of sins (1 Peter 4:8). People are often difficult to deal with. Therefore, unless our motivation to lead them is based on our love for God and for them, we may find that it decreases as the difficulty of our leadership increases. Labour without love tends towards legalism and harshness and it encourages striving, all of which are disastrous to our Christian walk, because they dry us up and sap our motivation. It is also important to know God's love experientially. Many Christian leaders are very insecure, and work hard day and night because they feel so unloved and uncertain of God's care for them. They feel that if they work hard enough and serve others selflessly enough, then they may earn God's love and approval. It must also be noted that powerful activity which is totally devoid of love is satanic. We need to avoid this at all costs.

Discipleship without cost

The gospel of Jesus Christ is freely available, but it is not cheap; in fact, it should cost us everything we are and have (as it did Jesus!). However, it is easier to get people to pray a prayer of commitment, than it is to bring people into a place of true discipleship. Jesus wants disciples, not decisions. People need to realise that accepting Jesus as their Lord and Saviour means, that from then on, He is Boss of their lives. They can no longer do just as they please. If we preach or believe in a discipleship without cost, we are going to have a rude shock, because true Christian discipleship can involve great cost to ourselves. So many new Christians are demotivated in their Christian walk and a vast number even drop out all together, because they hear a gospel that does not mention the suffering or the cost. Therefore, when these things inevitably arrive, they are totally unprepared for them and it causes them to fall (John 6:66). Jesus taught us first to weigh the cost before committing ourselves (Luke 14:25–35), and we need to make sure that those people with whom we share the gospel, know the cost of that to which they are going to commit their lives.

The key to salvation, however, is not that we believe we are saved, but that we believe we are loved by God. If we know that we are loved by a loving God, then we will know that we can trust Him and entrust our life into His hands, whatever the cost. Understanding this truth is essential, because it enables people to accept the cost of discipleship. Also, to have a discipleship without cost cheapens it, because the value of something is determined by the price people are willing to pay for it. If Christianity costs us everything, it will be the most important thing in our life.

To do what is right as a leader will cost us something, because it will usually mean that we will have to deny ourselves in some area. Leadership involves a competition between meeting the needs of those we lead and meeting our own needs. We need to be willing to pay this cost before we take up any form of leadership.

Leadership without followers

A true leader is like a shepherd in that they both have
followers. If you are a leader in name only, it will not take
you long to get frustrated and demotivated, because no one
will follow your leadership in the long-term. Some people
may follow you initially out of curiosity, loyalty or commitment, etc., but eventually this will wear off and you will be
left on your own. Leadership is something to which we are
called by God and it is something for which God equips us.
Taking up leadership in God's church outside of God's will is
dangerous both for ourselves and for those we are meant to
be leading. God chooses leaders who have a heart to do His
will. In fact, God's leaders need to be single-mindedly
committed to His will as they understand it. Double-minded
leaders gain few worthwhile followers.

Fellowship without unity

As Christians, we are all called to be part of the body of
Christ, the church (1 Corinthians 12:12–27). Jesus Himself
prayed for unity in His church just before He was crucified
(John 17:20–23). As we have seen, one of the reasons God
has given the five-fold ministry gifts to the church is to build
up the body of Christ until we all reach unity in the faith
and in the knowledge of the Son of God (Ephesians
4:12, 13). There are also many injunctions in the Scriptures
for Christians to love and encourage each other, because
these things cement God's church together and enable
unity. God is very concerned with unity in His church. As
part of His body, we should be working with all our might
for unity in the true church, as long as it does not compromise our walk with God or the truth of His Word (Romans
15:1–7; 1 Corinthians 1:10; Philippians 2:1–16). We can
have fellowship at least on the basis of our shared belief.
Where there is unity, it is there that the Lord commands the
blessing (Psalm 133:1–3). There is very little that will
demotivate us more than seeing fellow believers at logger-
heads with each other; or watching one believer pull

another down; or for us to be neglected for any reason. No wonder the second greatest commandment that Jesus gave to us was to love our neighbour as ourselves (Matthew 22:39).

Work without foresight

> *'It is not good to have zeal without knowledge, nor to be hasty and miss the way.'*   (Proverbs 19:2)

At the conclusion of any sustained period of intensive ministry, we are likely to end up with a spiritual hangover. Here we will feel drained and spent, and our supply of energy, which is usually available to keep us going, will have all but gone. Pastors tend to experience this condition every Monday morning. The reason for this phenomenon is that we cannot do work of a spiritual nature without energy going out from us (Luke 8:46). People drained in such a way often become negative, lonely, self-critical, and critical of other people. They tend to feel worthless and useless, and they amplify all the possible minor (and major!) errors they have made over recent days, i.e. they tend to get things out of perspective and generally feel sorry for themselves. The Christian experiencing such a state needs to meet with the Lord and allow Him to 'refuel' them spiritually and help them to see their situation (and their life) through His eyes. To rely on yesterday's motivation to get today's job done can leave us falling short of what is required and start the process of failure. We need to keep our eyes on God and at the same time look ahead and stay in a place of suitable preparedness for any situation we may encounter.

Our motivation to serve the Lord is most severely tested when we need to stand up against vigorous opposition. This type of opposition drains us quickly. We can only go on for so long, and then we will begin to lose our resistance and our resolve, unless we have a very close walk with God. What we need to do in these situations is to learn how to draw on God, and to meet daily with Him so that we are always prepared to meet these times of severe draining of our spiritual resources.

Sometimes when we are drained spiritually, our most pressing need is simply to withdraw and rest. Elijah, after his episode with the prophets of Baal on Mount Carmel, was totally drained of his spiritual resources. God knew what Elijah needed before anything else was sleep, food and a safe place in which to rest. Only after this did God start to deal with the spiritual problem (1 Kings 18:1–19:18).

It is also possible to be tired and drained in spirit, because we have not spent enough time with God over a long period. We are therefore empty inside. Multi-talented, hard-working people are very vulnerable to this lack of foresight, because they can work for quite a while in their own strength and they may not sense their need to spiritually 'refuel'. However, it is inevitable that one day things will begin to wrong for these people. They will reach a crisis point and find that they have not got the inner spiritual resource on which to draw that which they need. They will then realise how empty they really are and often this can give rise to feelings like rising turbulence, unexplained anxiety or panic, confused goals and motives, and inconsistent patterns of personal behaviour. These people may still be able to keep going out of habit and experience, but they will not really know God's peace or His power, their heart will not really be in their work, and they will not operate out of love. Often these people become very cynical and critical of others.

Church members today (especially Christian leaders), are confronted with a large number of church programmes, conferences and seminars etc. The competition for our time, energy and money grows more fierce with every passing year. Added to this is the bulk of information aimed at us through the church, television, radio and our general interaction with the world. All these inputs require filtering, sorting and decision-making and it has a wearing effect on us. What actually happens is that we get so much input from these things and we spend so much time doing our activities that we end up spending little or no time with God and being fed by Him. Eventually our eyes are drawn more to the world and our activities in it, than they are to the Lord. Human beings are like computers, to some extent, in that we become what we input. Our minds especially are trained and take their colour by what we input into them. The more we input from God, the more Christ-like we will become. Conversely, the more we input from the world, the more like it we will become. We need to make sure that the balance is tipped in favour of God in our lives. As Christians, we need to plug into our Source, God the Father. Unless we do this, we will not know what God's will is for our lives and, over the long-term, we will not have the inner resources we need in order to continue our work for the Lord. We will be sapped of our motivation to serve God as we should, and instead, we will begin to look to other areas of life to get our sense of enjoyment and fulfilment.

We all have days when we feel defeated, intimidated and/ or disheartened. These feelings tend to come on days when we know the taste of defeat or failure; or when we feel utterly impotent and unable to live up to our standards of faith; or we wonder how on earth what we are doing is going to come together; or we may simply no longer see the relevance of our faith to the world in which we live. Our motivation to serve the Lord tends to disappear when these feelings take root. At these times, we need to pick ourselves up and begin to seek the Lord. This is the only way to get things in the right perspective and to restore our resources in God.

> *'Those who wait on the Lord shall renew their strength; they shall mount up with wings like eagles, they shall run and not be weary, they shall walk and not faint.'*
>
> (Isaiah 40:31 NKJV)

Ministry without wisdom

Being with people can be exhausting. There are all kinds of people who come across our path each day. As we have seen, some will enable our motivation to serve the Lord, and we need to cultivate these friendships. On the other hand, some people will drain our motivation. This latter category of people tend to crowd our horizons as leaders in God's church, particularly in the areas of personal ministry and counselling. These people often simply want attention and they do not really care what state we are in once they have got what they want.

Jesus spent time with this type of person. He tried to help them and lift them to a higher level of maturity in God. However, the bulk of His time was spent with His heavenly Father and with His chosen disciples; and we, as His leaders, need to do the same. If we continually give in to the demands of people with problems, we will be rewarding and, therefore, reinforcing their negative behaviour by our attention and we will be encouraging these people to have an unhealthy dependence on us. We need to be loving but firm with these people. Unless we do this, we will grow very tired and this can cause us eventually to become disillusioned, embittered people who, given half a chance, would give up. Our motivation to serve the Lord will decrease day by day, if we always respond to the pressures other people place on us, instead of living as the Lord intends us to live.

Jesus taught us to go the extra mile (Matthew 5:38–42), and He lived out this teaching in His own life. Even when He was very tired, He always seemed to be able to give Himself to other people and meet their needs. However, Jesus knew how to draw on His Father at all times, and how to stay in tune with Him. He was always doing His Father's will and, there-fore, He was in the right place at the right time. He also knew how to keep ministry short and still meet the needs of the people who came to Him. This still left Him vast amounts of time to spend with His Father and His disciples. The very pace of life in those days also enabled Him to do this. God's leaders today need to make sure that they do not cut people off from their attention. At times, they will need to give until it hurts. However, it is wrong to give until it wipes us out, so that we cannot do the things we know God would have us concentrate on.

People without hope

> *'Let us hold fast the confession of our hope without wavering, for he who promised is faithful.'*   (Hebrews 10:23 NKJV)

Shattered expectations or failed dreams can cause us to live a life without hope in the world. This condition often leads to a severe loss of motivation, and it causes some people to give up and others to go through some form of mental break-down (Proverbs 13:12). Fortunately, this condition is usually found outside God's family. However, in today's high pace, high pressure world, even Christians, who take their eyes off the Lord and who look to the world for their source of hope and fulfilment, can find themselves in this tragic state of feeling hopeless. Christians in this position need to get their eyes back on Jesus and realise afresh the hope they have in Him. If we keep our eyes fixed on Jesus, whatever is happening around us or to us, and if we live as we should in God, we will know a hope that will not fail us (Romans 5:3–5; Hebrews 6:11, 17–20).

Faith without deeds

> *'As the body without the spirit is dead, so faith without deeds is dead.'*   (James 2:26)

If we try to live a life of faith without deeds, we will find that our motivation to serve the Lord will soon suffer, because faith is meant to be outworked (James 2:14–26). In fact, faith will die without the opportunity for it to be expressed.

Exercises

1. Go through the questions in the introduction to this chapter and answer them honestly. What do your answers reveal about yourself? What motivates you to serve the Lord? Are all your sources of motivation right? What are you going to do about it?

2. Answer the questions in the section entitled 'Drive without Discernment'. What drives you to do what you do? Is there anything which needs to change in this area?

3. Have you obeyed every word the Lord has spoken to you? Why not? Do you trust your discernment in this area? Has it improved over recent years? Do you find that you hear less or more from God now, than you did in the past? How important is it that you hear from God? How important is it to your leadership? Should it be more important?

Chapter 4

Dealing with Negatives

> *It is possible for Christians to overcome/
> avoid those negatives which plague the
> lives of people in the world.*

Introduction

There are many negatives which any Christian has to
overcome in order to live life as God intends. Some of these
negatives are particularly a problem for Christian leaders.
The following chapter is not designed to be a complete list
of these negatives, but rather to be a help that God's leaders
can use in order to notice and overcome/avoid some of the
more destructive and demotivating of them.

Competition

Christians today do live in a fiercely competitive world, and
this spirit of competition has entered into church life. God
has called His people to work together as part of the world-
wide body of Christ. Unfortunately, some Christians see
other people, who should be their partners and fellow
workers in the Kingdom of God, as threats. Pastors fight
with feelings of ill-will towards another whose congregation
is larger; preachers compare another's public acceptance to

their own; and church members all compete to get the best leadership positions in their churches. When a competitive spirit takes root, everybody else's success becomes a threat to our own. This is a dangerous position to be in, because we will always be looking sideways at the path that others are taking, instead of keeping our eyes on the Lord and following the path that He has chosen for us to walk. A competitive spirit breeds distrust of other people, especially those in similar positions to us, and it causes us to make only shallow relationships with these people. Competition also introduces paranoia and great insecurity into a church, and wherever it takes root it tends to negate the peace of God and destroy unity. All these things are very demotivating for the Christian who is seeking to live a righteous, holy life and who wants to obey God wholeheartedly.

Criticism

This is when we find it easy to see the problems and difficulties in the church (and in everything else we encounter), and we enjoy sharing these with other people. It is the tendency to emphasize the negative in every situation; to major on the ideological or doctrinal differences at the expense of everything else that is said; to see the character fault and not the rest of the person; and to concentrate on locating the weaknesses in a programme, instead of finding the answers. Leaders often fall into this trap when they see other leaders doing something that they do not think is right. Critical people tend to spend so much time criticising that they run out of time and energy to actually solve the problems and get the job done. These people look at everything with a critical eye and they cannot often even see the positive. Such criticism tends to nullify any motivation to serve the Lord that we might once have had, mainly because we cannot see how a job with so many faults could be achieved.

Christians need to learn how to cope in God's way with the criticism of other people; and not react with bitterness or resentment, but rather with forgiveness as Jesus taught us to do (Matthew 6:14, 15). The criticism may hurt, but it is better out in the open than behind our back. It is virtually impossible to be in a place of leadership and not receive some criticism, if we are doing our job properly. When we do receive any form of criticism, we should not overreact, especially if it is in an area in which we know we are weak. We should stay calm, and then honestly assess what has been said in order to establish in our heart whether it is true or not. We then need to commit the problem to God and make sure that we never entertain any thought of revenge in our heart (Proverbs 20:22). Remember, there is usually a small amount of truth in every criticism; if we can find this truth and learn from it, we will be the better person for it (Psalm 141:5; Proverbs 25:12).

Vanity

This is when we want people to prefer or like us and we dare not do anything which might jeopardize this. This inner need to be admired usually arises from our own insecurities. Here, the desire to impress other people overcomes or at best compromises our motivation to serve the Lord in His way and in His time. As Christians, we need to seek our approval from God and not from other people.

Ambition

This is the urge to get ahead and to establish ourselves powerfully and securely. It is the force that gets us to climb over and manipulate other people in order for us to get to the top, no matter what effect this has on other people. Ambition wants fame, reputation, success and power and the rewards that go with these things, and it weighs every situation in order to achieve those ends. Once we are caught in ambition's web, we will seize every opportunity in which to prove ourselves and our gifts. Ambitious people try to impress other people by name dropping and are more concerned with position than they are with other people and servanthood. Cultivating an image often becomes a priority in ambitious people's lives. This only serves to channel their attention and energy away from others and towards themselves. Such people fear letting other people see who they really are, because they are trying to make those people see something different. These people also have to work very hard to maintain this image and keep up the pretence. This may necessitate them to having to lie and cheat on a regular basis. In fact, these people are continually trying to prove themselves to other people (e.g. boast that they are at least one better than those they lead).

Our service for the Lord will take on twisted motives if ambition is not kept in check. In fact, ambition will drain our motivation to serve the Lord, because we will never be satisfied with where we are at, what we have, or what we are doing (Philippians 2:3, 4). It is alright to want to improve ourselves or to aspire to leadership, but we should only do so for the right reasons, i.e. to bring glory to God and to enable His work to be done. If we have an overwhelming ambition to be 'somebody', then we will focus too much on that and not enough on serving other people (and helping them to become somebodies).

Pride

This could be defined, in Christian terms, as the inability to handle the popularity, success, position or gifts with which we have been entrusted by God (1 Corinthians 4:7; 2 Corinthians 10:12, 13). It is a condition where we put ourselves first and we are what matters most. Here, the applause and adulation intoxicate, seduce and blind us, and this becomes our motivation to do what we do. Our motivation is to serve and even enthrone ourselves rather than the Lord. This is the trap that caused the downfall of Lucifer. The very fact that we have risen to a position of leadership can breed a secret self-congratulation and pride. The only way out of this pitfall is to humble ourselves under the mighty hand of God and let Him raise us up in His time (1 Peter 5:6). Leaders need to watch out for and stop any exaggerated deference other people may give to them. It is too easy to let such praise and adulation go to our head and result in pride (Ecclesiastes 7:5). Leaders should be esteemed and respected, but they should never be put on a pedestal and idolised. Instead, leaders should deflect any praise and adulation they may get to the Lord (James 4:1–10). If people do put us on a pedestal, their expectations of us can be very high and very hard for any leader to maintain. This introduces a tremendous tension and restriction into a leader's life, because the leader knows that those who have put them on a pedestal could reject them the moment they see the slightest imperfection. Leaders need to avoid this at all costs.

Failure

Even God-called, Spirit-filled, Spirit-led and empowered leaders fail and make mistakes at times. We must never think of ourselves as infallible, even if we have prayed about something more than everybody else or we are usually right. On the other hand, we must never let failure cause us to give up or to demotivate us for any length of time. If we fail by falling into sin, we need to confess it and get right with God (1 John 1:9); and then forgive ourselves and not indulge in self-pity or self-condemnation. If our failure is related to our leadership or ministry, e.g. failing to achieve goals, incorrect discernment when ministering etc., we need to go to God and commit the problem to Him. He may reveal something to us that makes our failure easier to accept or He may show us what we need to do next. Our failures may hurt, but we must not let them be blown out of all proportion in our mind and so dominate our thinking and our emotions. Once the sting has gone out of the failure, we should look to see if there is anything we can do to improve the situation. If not, we need to learn from the experience, and then put it behind us and get on with life. Failure may cause us to have to start all over again, but at least we can learn from our experience; and God willing, we will do a better job for Him next time. Many leaders distance themselves from their past mistakes and failures by becoming cynical. If this takes root in our lives, it can be devastating to our hope, courage and motivation to serve the Lord.

Christians should not like failure, but they should not fear it. If we are afraid to fail, we will never be really fruitful for God, because we will never take the risks, confront the challenges or be creative in the way needed for this. The truth is that mistakes and failure are not the obstacles, but the fear of them is. Rising above failures and mistakes is essential if we are going to stay motivated in our service for the Lord. We need to learn how to forgive ourselves for our failures, so that we can approach new goals with clarity of mind and conscience.

Success

In some ways, success is more difficult to handle than failure, because it is intoxicating and it encourages pride (which can so easily destroy us). We need to remember that success in the work of God is the result of God at work and, therefore, all the glory needs to go to Him. Leadership should only be undertaken in God's Kingdom at His request and it should only be carried out to bring glory to Him. It is wrong to take on Christian leadership as a tool to achieve our own personal ambitions, to increase our prestige, or to enable our advancement. We need to have God's motives and His glory in mind only. This may have to be our aim at the beginning of our lives as one of God's leaders, because God may not have yet uncovered many of the attitude problems that we harbour deep inside of us.

Jealousy

Jealous people covet the success, gift or possessions of other people so much that it begins to affect them, their actions and their motives. They want what other people have. As Christian leaders, we should be jealous only for God and so give Him all the glory at all times. This then leaves no room for us to be jealous of other people. We also need to learn to live and minister in the limits God has set for us, and to bless others who are gifted by Him.

Indispensability

It is a big mistake to think of ourselves as irreplaceable or as the only person God could possibly use for a job (Romans 12:3). The truth is that it is God who accomplishes the work and He can do so without us. Many older leaders, in particular, have trouble in this area and they, therefore, cling to their office long after they should have passed it on to other younger men (whom they should have trained to do the work). This has been the cause of so many organisations which started well, falling into decay. Leaders can lead in such a way that people become dependent on them (usually this is motivated by insecurity, pride, and the need to be needed and appreciated); or they can lead in a way that causes people to depend on the Lord, while at the same time training another person to take up their role as leader in the future. This is the only way to ensure the long-term success of any work for the Lord. To be possessive about a work and to quench the potential of any who could possibly take our place of leadership, is to hinder the work of God. We may have started a work and we may be the best person available to lead a work, but the truth is that it is God's work and, if we let Him, He can raise up a leader to replace us, even as He raised us up.

Inferiority and loneliness

Inferiority is self-doubt about who we are and what we can do. If the enemy succeeds in making us feel inferior, we will tend to conform and fit into what other people want, so that they will love and accept us. Fear of rejection is a powerful motivation to such people. Inferiority also causes people to draw in on themselves and even isolate themselves from other people. A person suffering from this will find that they cannot lead other people effectively.

It is often very lonely being a leader and this can cause us great hurt, at times. Lonely leaders often protect themselves by keeping in with people. They, therefore, avoid saying anything that may be unpopular; avoid rebuking those who need it; conform to what other people expect of them; give other people what they want; and often use the 'poor me' technique to gain other people's attention, affirmation and sympathy. In fact, many leaders who suffer from inferiority, insecurity or loneliness surround themselves with people who always support and agree with them (i.e. yes men). Of course, leaders should avoid causing unnecessary offence, but they need to remember that they are in the business of doing God's will and bringing people into maturity in Christ. To aim just to make people feel good and to accept our leadership (i.e. meeting our need to be liked and accepted) is to miss out on what God has called us to do as His leaders. Achieving popularity by compromise may be easy, but it will eventually destroy our spiritual ministry. Remember, our value as a leader does not depend on other people liking or esteeming us, it depends on God and the way He views us. The truth is that He loves us and wants only our best. Our worth in God's sight is settled and we can rest secure in this. We do not need to prove ourselves, or look good to other people, we just need to do what is right by obeying God and serving Him lovingly and wholeheartedly (2 Corinthians 10:12–18; 1 Thessalonians 2:4–6).

Guilt

Guilt, whether real or imagined, can motivate us to work for our salvation, because we feel we owe a debt to God or humanity and we need to work it out. In fact, this can cause us to work very hard and even wear ourselves out, without really knowing why. To be motivated by guilt can lead to a very unhappy life which never finds fulfilment, because guilt is never satisfied. God wants us to know His forgiveness, acceptance and love, and to live a life that is free of guilt.

Fear

This is a very powerful motivating force. It can cause us to forget what we know to be right and to do things we will regret. Fear can even be aroused simply by the way we are thinking, e.g. thinking about the unknown, rejection, or failure. This fear can cause us as leaders to distance ourselves from those we lead in order to protect ourselves and avoid hurt and rejection. Fearful leaders often refuse to open themselves up to other people, because they have decided that getting close to others can cause them too much pain. These leaders keep people at an arms length and give their attention and commitment instead to the tasks that need to be done. Unfortunately, these leaders have forgotten that leadership is more about people than work, especially in God's church. Leaders need to love their people and give selflessly to them. This is true even for prophets, teachers and administrators, who most commonly suffer from this problem. We need to get close to those we lead, if we want to be effective leaders. This may mean that other people see our faults, but we should not let fear of this cause us to distance ourselves from those we lead. Equipping other people for service in God's Kingdom is enabled by relationships, not a set of detailed rules handed out by a distant leader.

Over-caution is often the result of a fear-filled life. Over-cautious, fearful people tend to have nothing but financial and health problems. Nothing goes right for them, because they are too afraid to enter into anything wholeheartedly. They avoid anything that hints of risk and so are rarely creative or successful.

> 'Let the record books show you won, or let it show you lost, but don't let it show you failed to play the game!'
>
> (Jim Rohn)

We need to remember that, as Christians, God has not given to us a spirit of fear, but of power and of love and of a sound mind (2 Timothy 1:7 NKJV).

Doubt and pessimism

If we continue to think negative thoughts, and allow doubt to become unbelief instead of faith, we will find ourselves becoming totally demoralised, demotivated and disillusioned with our Christian life. In fact, depression and the things associated with it, are the only end result of such pessimistic thinking which goes on for long enough.

Laziness and complacency

These will both rob us of our motivation and our drive to obey God and see His will carried out, especially if we are lazy in our times with God and His Word (Proverbs 18:9; 2 Thessalonians 3:6–15). There is no place for laziness or complacency in the Kingdom of God. We need to guard against these things by seeing our life and our work as God does. He sees us as His sons whom He loves, and those to whom He has entrusted His will. Like the apostle Paul, we need to press on until we finish the work God has set out before us (Philippians 3:12–14).

Indifference and indecision

Indifference breeds fatalism and causes us not to care what happens. This only succeeds in robbing us of any form of success. It also results in indecision which is the thief of opportunity. As Christians, we need to make the most of every opportunity (Galatians 6:10; Ephesians 5:15,16; Colossians 4:5). This is the only way to know the abundant life that Jesus promised (John 10:10 NKJV).

Conclusion

There are probably many other negatives which you can think of that will demotivate a Christian and hinder the effectiveness of their service for the Lord. However, the negatives mentioned above are a good starting point to study, so that you will not fall into the pitfalls into which many other Christian leaders have already fallen. To keep motivated is an essential part of our Christian walk. Too many Christians, the moment things start to get tough, pull out of the running and give up. We desperately need to determine what motivates us and what keeps us motivated, so that we are prepared in any situation, no matter how difficult or costly, to do God's will.

> *'Not that I have already obtained all this, or have already been made perfect, but I press on to take hold of that for which Christ Jesus took hold of me. Brothers, I do not consider myself yet to have taken hold of it. But one thing I do: Forgetting what is behind and straining towards what is ahead, I press on towards the goal to win the prize for which God has called me heavenwards in Christ Jesus.'* (Philippians 3:12–14)

The apostle Paul had a lot to forget. In the past, he had behaved appallingly towards the faith he now confessed, and had fought for all he was worth against Him who was now His Lord. Later, however, Paul became one of the most motivated Christians ever known. He may have failed early in life, but he was determined to put that behind him and do everything he possibly could to serve God. He was willing to do anything that God asked of Him, whatever the cost. As disciples of Jesus, we need to find out what God wants us to do, and then get on and do it in God's way and in His time. If we continually look to God, He will provide us with everything that is necessary to motivate us into action and keep us motivated, until we complete the task that He has set for us to do (Philippians 4:19; 2 Peter 1:3). Keeping our eyes on the Lord and staying close to Him will also help us to avoid the enemies of motivation that will inevitably try to trip us up. Then we, like Paul, will be able to do whatever God asks of us, whatever the cost to ourselves.

Exercises

1. Do you recognise brilliance in other people and wonder why God has so gifted them, when those gifts could be

used so well by you? Is your service for God stifled by the way you compare yourself with other people? Do you fear those in your group, who, if they reached their full potential, would outshine you? Does your personal prestige mean more to you than the development of those in your group?

2. Does willingness to concede the possibility of error of judgement and to prefer, at times, the assessment of other people to our own, increase or decrease our influence with other people? Why is this so? Do you do this as a leader? Have you created an open climate in which other people can tell you honestly whether you are doing a good job as a leader, or not? Are those you lead frightened to tell you anything negative about you? Is an open climate a good idea?

3. There are a number of questions we can ask ourselves in order to test for pride. How do you react when someone is raised up over you? How do you react when other people are praised in your presence or when they outshine you in gift or accomplishment? How do you feel and how do you react when other people criticise you? Do you think more highly of yourself, your accomplishments and your import-ance than you ought? Do you consider everything in relation to yourself and its effect on you, or do you consider God and other people first? Do you hold in contempt anyone less gifted than you? How strong is your need to be noticed and admired?

4. Not all your ideals for God's work will be realised. How do you react when things go wrong? How do you react when people you trust fail you, especially if it is at a time when you really need them? When you are successful, to whom do you give the glory? Are you manipulating people or events in order to put yourself in a good light or to make yourself needed? Are you aware of a competitive spirit that encour-ages you or others to jostle for position or status? What should you do about it? Does your position of leadership or power give you your sense of self-worth?

5. Having read this chapter, you have probably been challenged in many areas. Go to God, yield your life afresh to Him; and then ask Him to reveal anything to you that needs to change. Do not put it off! It is very important that our motivation to serve the Lord is right. Many Christian leaders do a lot of damage, because they fail to take the time to wait on God and examine their lives with Him. The Holy Spirit will not only show us the things that need to change, He will help us to change them.

Chapter 5

Motivating Other People

> *Motivation is infectious –*
> *if you have it, then it is likely to spread*
> *to those you lead, eventually!*

Introduction

To motivate other people is to infuse them with a spirit of willingness or eagerness to perform effectively and, therefore, to accomplish the work that needs to be done. The best way for leaders to do this is to be such motivated people themselves, that others will be inspired by their example, i.e. they should seek to be a model/pacesetter by doing those things that they want the people who follow them to be doing. In fact, a Christian leader's life should motivate other people to serve God more effectively. Christian leaders should also learn to be excited and enthusiastic about their work, because these qualities are contagious.

Motivation is sourced in the individual. Leaders, therefore, cannot create self-motivation in other people, but they can create a set of circumstances that encourages motivation. Good leaders know how to spark motivation and keep it aflame in every individual that they lead. They know how to get people to work because they want to and not because they are forced to (because the former is the only way to get effective, enduring service). Christian leaders always need to remember though that they mainly lead volunteers (who can walk out at any time), and that they are leading on God's behalf. They should therefore only use biblical and appropriate ways to encourage the people they lead to grow in God and serve Him.

The way people think and act is caused

There is never only one cause for any given behaviour. Behaviour can be caused by a number of complex things, e.g. how the person sees themselves, what the person's environment is like, how the person perceives their situation, what the person's values are, what the person needs/ wants at the time etc. However, if a leader can recognise what makes a person do what they do, then they will be one step closer toward providing the right set of circumstances to enable the person to be (and stay) motivated. Remember, God's leaders should only be motivating their people to become more like Jesus and to do God's will.

A person's behaviour is greatly influenced by what they value (i.e. what they believe in and to what they have committed themselves). It is part of the Christian leader's task to help the people they lead to reject worldly values and overcome worldly influences (which will cause them to be motivated towards worldly pursuits), and instead to yield/ commit their lives to God (and therefore be motivated to obey Him and be His disciple). Leaders also need to remember that what they do makes a very large difference to the motivation of the people they lead.

When motivating other people, leaders need to remember that each of those people has a mind, emotions and a will (which are collectively known as the soul). The mind recognises and deals with facts; the emotions give us certain feelings which are the result of knowing the facts; and the will determines what action we will take as a result of knowing the facts and feeling the way we do about them.

All these three parts of the soul need to be taken into consideration when we are seeking to motivate other people effectively.

Needs regulate our behaviour

Most people's behaviour is largely controlled/regulated by their selfish needs. Unsatisfied needs tend to dominate people and organise their behaviour until those needs are fulfilled (because once a need is satisfied it disappears). Needs can be split into four categories (this is a modified version of the research findings of psychologist, Abraham Maslow):

1. **The need to survive**
   These are the most dominant needs like eating, drinking, sleeping, and safety which deal with subsistence/survival. They are all relatively independent of each other, but they are needs which so demand to be met that they will usually override all other needs.

2. **The need to be wanted, loved and belong**
   These needs represent the desire to be accepted by a group and the desire for affection. These needs only tend to be important once the survival needs are met.

3. **The need for self-esteem**
   This is the need to know the feeling of adequacy/security that comes from accomplishment, achievement, having position/status, and being appreciated by other people. This need only tends to arise when we feel wanted, loved and accepted by other people and our survival needs are met.

4. **The need for self-fulfilment**
   This is the need to become everything that we want and are capable of becoming. This need only tends to arise once all the other needs have been met. However, this is the highest level of attainment possible, and for the Christian it should represent all that God wants them to be and do.

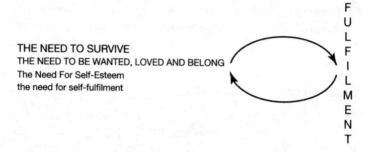

Figure 1   *The Need/Fulfilment Vicious Cycle.*

Many Christians are caught in the vicious cycle of need fulfilment (see Figure 1), which starts with a felt need and ends with its fulfilment (in which the majority of human-kind is trapped). This cycle causes even the Christian to live a self-centred, unfruitful life. It also explains, to some degree, why many Christians (at times) have such a low inner drive to do what they know God would have them do, i.e. they want to become and do what God wants, but they are trapped in some part of the need/fulfilment vicious cycle (usually lower down where the strongest pressure for fulfil-ment exists, e.g. the need for food or the need to be loved). Until the person's more basic needs are met, they will not be motivated to achieve any of their higher needs. Of course, there is not a rigid hierarchy of needs which always have to be met in this order. The reason we include this need/ fulfilment vicious cycle here is that it does give leaders an insight into why some people fail to respond to their attempts to motivate them spiritually (e.g. a person's concern for God's work and growth in maturity in Him may be swamped by their need to be loved and accepted).

Christian leaders need to understand where the people they lead are at, in terms of their needs, in order to motivate them. Trying to motivate a starving person to lead a Sunday School class will be difficult (James 2:14–20); whereas offer-ing bread or second-hand clothes to a Western business man is not going to open them up to the gospel. God's leaders need to meet their people where they are at and help them to meet any of their basic needs (when possible) (i.e. feed them when they are hungry, clothe them when naked, go to them when they are in prison, etc.: Matthew 25:31–46; James 2:14–18). This process may be time consuming, demanding and costly, but it will enable the leader to take the person on and start to meet some of their spiritual needs. To ignore a person's basic needs will usually cause the leader to fail to achieve anything very much of value in terms of that person's spiritual growth and maturity. People need to be helped to overcome any need/fulfilment vicious cycle in which they are caught, so that they can go on in God and begin to live in a way that is God-centred rather than self-centred.

You get what you reward

People in the world today tend to behave as the reward system teaches them to behave (i.e. they withhold their best efforts when they can see little relationship between what they do and how they are rewarded, and they give their best when they can see that there is something in it for them). This may sound wrong to the Christian, but even we respond to rewards (because we, like most other people, tend to do the things that benefit us the most). Of course, there are many other things which determine a person's performance (e.g. personal ability, needs, values, etc.), but rewards are very important in determining behaviour and they, therefore, must be considered when thinking about the whole concept of motivating other people.

Many people in leadership confuse activity with efficiency or productivity and, as a result, they reward activities regardless of their value, e.g. they financially reward the person who works for 10 hours, the same or more than they reward the person who does the same amount of work in half the time (the end result of which tends to be that the hard working person works less hard). As we can see from this example, it is easy to reward the wrong activities and punish/ignore the right ones. So often this is the main reason that leaders fail to motivate their people to do what they want them to do. If leaders are not getting the results that they want, they should ask themselves, 'What behaviour am I rewarding?'

People a leader should reward

- People who seek God for His vision for a team/church and stick with this until it is completed.

- Peacemakers and encouragers, because these people:
  - help unite a team; enable disputes to be settled quickly (disputes destroy unity and slow down the work);
  - encourage those who need it; and
  - enable the job to be done (because they are constantly motivating their team mates to work hard so that the team's God-given goals are achieved).

- People who are innovative and creative, especially where this enables team goals to be achieved more effectively. This has to be encouraged, because most churches/organisations resist any change (they would rather have security). Leaders need to create a team climate that facilitates innovation and growth.

- Any person who does their work with excellence, because this brings glory to God (remember though that the end does not justify the means in the Kingdom of God). Doing things excellently is simply a matter of attitude and commitment. Remember, doing it right the first time is better than doing it fast and sloppy. This is because:
  - quality is improved;
  - we are learning by our mistakes and correcting them as we go;
  - less checking will be required next time;
  - team members have greater job satisfaction (because they know that they have done something well, etc.); and
  - when we do something fast and sloppy, it often is done wrongly and this necessitates our having to do it again.

- People who bring suggestions for the improvement of their job/service for the Lord. Leaders need to realise that the people closest to the job usually know the most about it. Leaders also need to learn that they do not always have the all the answers and they do not have to make all the decisions.

- People who are involved in team activities. Of course, team members who are working well on their own should be rewarded, but leaders need to make sure that these individuals know/are aware that their contribution is part of the team's overall goals/vision. Remember, a team's success depends on all the team members working together towards achieving commonly held goals/aims/etc. Team members should therefore not be encouraged to work against each other or to criticise each other. The best thing to do is to remove rewards that encourage too much individual effort and to instead set goals (with corresponding rewards) which can only be achieved when the team works together.

- Good high-achieving workers. Of course, as Christian leaders, we should encourage everybody we lead to do better. However, we need to make sure that we reward those who work hard and never ignore them, because otherwise these people may lose motivation/heart and we will have lost the people whom we need the most to achieve team goals/vision/etc. Rewarding hard workers will also help to motivate those who do not work as hard, because the latter group will see the leadership affirm and spend time with those who are putting in the effort and doing well. Most people do not mind working hard, but they do not like having their efforts taken for granted. This makes them feel used, frustrated, exploited, discouraged and unappreciated, and they tend to complain by slowing down, withholding effort, or giving up. Curt Bergwall once said, 'The greatest ability is dependability.' Leaders need to make an effort to locate these dependable, hard-working workers, because they often are the people who get on with the job quietly and so are easily overlooked. This is well worth the leader's effort, because it will reinforce this person's behaviour and encourage other people to do the same. Some questions you can ask to discover these people include:

– Who are rarely missing from work?
– Who are willing to give more when the team needs it?
– Who are always there when you need them?
– Who can you rely on when the going gets tough?
– Who can you count on to fill in for someone else when needed?
– Who gets on with their job without bothering the leadership, unless necessary?
– Who work just as well if the leadership are there or not?
– Who help other people to do their job better?
– Who increase team morale/motivation/unity/co-operation?
– Who produce more answers than problems?
– Who are continually trying to improve what they are doing for the Lord?
– Who want to be held accountable for what they do?
– Who do not complain (in order to get attention)?

Somebody once said that any organisation contains four types of bones: wishbones (who wish that someone else would do the work); jawbones (who talk a lot but do little else); knucklebones (who knock what everybody else does); backbones (who get down and actually do the work). Leaders should only encourage/reward the latter group.

• People who are loyal and committed. There are two main ways that loyalty and commitment are gained from people, i.e. when the people know that their leaders are loyal and committed to them, and by rewarding it. Leaders should only want the best for the people they lead and they should make sure that their people know this (because then they will tend to get the best out of their people). Other helps in this area are: having open management (because people want to know that their leaders care enough about them to be available to them and be willing to listen to them when needed); showing no favouritism or unfairness; making sure that everyone in the team clearly knows the objectives/goals to which they are aiming (i.e. create and keep open, good, effective communication channels); providing job security when appropriate; training and developing your people and letting them know that you want as many of them as possible to become the team's future leadership, or at least to take on greater responsibility within the team.

Ways a Christian leader can reward good work

- Increased responsibility. This important reward should only be granted in God's Kingdom when He calls the person to leadership or greater responsibility. Remember, never raise a person up just because they have been around for a long time or because they work hard.

- Appropriate recognition, affirmation, praise, and encouragement. These are very important rewards a Christian leader can give those who work with/for them. People need to know that they are wanted and appreciated (Proverbs 15:23). When you do compliment/affirm those who deserve it, do it with sincerity. Remember, your attitude toward other people will affect (and sometimes determine) the way they feel about you! If leaders honour and serve those they lead, then those people are far more likely to honour and serve their leaders. The encouragement of a leader also helps to give people a sense of self-worth. Goethe once said,

  'If you treat a man as he is, he will stay as he is. But if you treat him as if he were what he ought to be, and could be, he will become that bigger and better man.'

Leaders need to expect the best from those they lead and they will get it as long as they are realistic. Remember though not to praise every little thing that is done, because this will give your praise less meaning. Remember also to give credit where it is due. Someone once said,

> 'You can do just about anything you want if you don't care who gets the credit.'

- Giving people jobs that they enjoy doing. This is an especially good reward for hard working, efficient, effective workers. Remember, people tend to enjoy doing the things that they do best.

- Increasingly involving people in the decision-making process. This shows that you notice the people, recognise their importance, and trust their opinion. Leaders and team members need to work together, not against each other. Remember, people will support what they helped to create; and change occurs faster and is longer lasting when it is accompanied by a high degree of worker participation at the decision-making level.

- Giving people the opportunity to advance themselves by paying for them to go on courses relevant to their field (or in areas the person would like to learn more about). This gives the team member the opportunity to learn new skills, and therefore be able to expand their job-field and improve their ability to do the job.

- Giving people challenging, stretching assignments. This helps the team member to learn by experience. Offering exciting, pace-setting challenges will attract highly motivated people to the team (and keep them on it).

- Giving people more freedom to make decisions, to create and find new and better answers, and to do things the way they want to do them, i.e. let the people be their own bosses as much as possible (while still being accountable to the leadership for their performance). When the right people are allowed to be creative, to plan and dream, it encourages their dedication and it inspires their motivation and effort (whereas otherwise they would be bored and dissatisfied). Remember, questions are a good way to stimulate imagination. Leaders may feel that they are losing control when they give their people independence/freedom, but trying to keep a talented, motivated person in a tightly controlled box will end up demotivating that person or even driving them away.

- Financial support: for most Christian workers, money is not the prime consideration, but it needs to be considered when the team member is a full-time Christian worker. No one can give their best if they are always concerned about where their finance is coming from, especially if they have a family. Of course, Christian workers should look to God for their provision, but God usually looks to humans to provide for His servants. A labourer is worthy of his hire according to the Bible (Luke 10:7; 1 Timothy 5:18). A church should therefore provide comfortably for those who lead them on a full-time basis. In fact, they should bless those who are willing to give up much in order to serve the Lord. Remember though, Christians should never link their performance to the level of their wages, i.e. they should not be serving God for the money.

- Other rewards: there are an endless number of creative ways of rewarding people. Leaders need to try and work out what rewards work best with their people and which ones produce the behaviour/work practice that they desire. For example, a way to reward good work or exceptional service is to give the person a day (or a few days) off. This can be accompanied by something like money for a meal out, or some theatre tickets, or even a holiday package. When you give unusual or exceptional rewards, make sure you do it in a way that enables the rest of the team to see the wisdom of it (they will then be able to rejoice with the people rather than be envious or jealous). Leaders can also let team members who finish their work go home early (this helps discourage those who take too long to do a job).

Satisfiers versus dissatisfiers

Frederick Herzberg has discovered from research that there are certain factors which increase a person's satisfaction with their work (and therefore their productivity), which all relate to the work that person does, i.e. achievement, recognition, the work itself, responsibility, and advancement. If these things are absent, Herzberg discovered that the person became apathetic rather than dissatisfied. Herzberg also discovered a range of different factors which increase a person's dissatisfaction with their work, which tended to relate more to job context or the environment out of which the job emerges, i.e. bad interpersonal relationships (especially between the person and their superiors/peers), inadequate technical ability of supervisor, poor company policy and administration, poor working conditions, and unsatisfactory personal life off the job. Note, the research showed that the absence of dissatisfiers did not necessarily make the person happy on the job.

Many of these principles relate to Christian work as well. Christian leaders seeking to motivate those they lead should try to emphasize the satisfiers and wipe out the dissatisfiers, because the latter are destroying their team members morale/motivation.

Other methods a Christian leader can use to help team members become more effective/motivated

- Making sure that the right person is doing the right job. Team members who do not have the ability or capacity to do a job will waste enormous amounts of their time and energy (and other team members time and energy) trying to do something that they are not cut out (or called by God) to do. Remember though that sometimes the problem is that the person has been given a poor job description, they are inadequately trained, or they do not have the necessary resources (or tools) they need to do the job.

- Sincerely demonstrating their concern and care for the people they lead, i.e. be conscious of their needs, ambitions, fears, and who they are as people. Cold, insensitive, impersonal, disinterested, indifferent leaders, tend to find it very hard to get any extra effort from those people they lead. Remember, leaders need to love and care for those they lead. In fact, people should matter far more than policies/procedure/organisation/ goal achievement/etc. Leaders should also never seem to be preoccupied with their own interests or only 'pretend' to be interested in those they lead. If people suspect that we, as leaders, are using them to accomplish our own needs, their willingness to follow us will rapidly decline.

- Treating team members and the people they lead in the way they would want to be treated. Leaders, at times, need to put themselves in the shoes of the people they lead. This will help to prevent them from pushing the people they lead around or demanding unearned respect/obedience/etc.

- Making sure that all team members have everything (within reason) that they need in order to do their job effectively (this may necessitate replacing old worn out equipment with new, more efficient equipment, or spending more money on resource materials, etc.).

- Helping workers, especially those in leadership positions, to realise/recognise the importance of their position. This can be done from the pulpit, through church training programmes, and by personally speaking to people (public recognition is a good way to prove the worth of a position to the rest of the congregation/ organisation). It can also be done by introducing special events like: taking all the workers/leaders out for a meal once a year, having a dedication service (perhaps involving the laying on of hands), or personal letters of recognition from the pastor etc.

- Giving sincere appreciation. This is a very important part of helping workers know they are recognised, especially when they have done something that is deserving of appreciation (serving selflessly without being noticed can be very demotivating and can cause workers to feel they are being taken for granted). Leaders who recognise effort are far more likely to get more effort from those they lead (this is especially important when people are doing work on their leader's behalf). Note, recognising what our superiors do and affirming them not only helps to motivate them, but it also tends to motivate these people to do more for us. All recognition is meaningful, no matter how brief. Remember, if no one asks about a person's work (or shows any form of interest in it), that person will probably begin to wonder if it really needs to be done at all!

- Making sure that potential workers/leaders see the various positions they could take up in the church as a privilege. In fact, God's people should want to serve Him in the various positions the church can provide. This will necessitate making those positions something with which the person will want to identify. The best way to do this is to educate church members so that they recognise the importance and privilege of any Christian service/job.

- Setting high (but reasonable) standards. Christian leaders need to realise that no one really wants to be associated with a shoddy, poorly organised enterprise. They also need to communicate standards which are consistent and fair, because then the people they lead will know that they have a stable target at which to aim. At times, high standards will seem to hinder the recruitment of church workers, but eventually it will lead to better workers who are held in higher esteem by the rest of the congregation.

- Keeping people well informed, especially about changes which affect them. Appropriate information serves as a motivating agent to help people to achieve. No one will be helped if we, as leaders, always hide things from everyone. On the other hand, if we, as leaders, tell people about team needs and we clarify team objectives, we can often get a boost in team and individual motivation. For example, motivation can be boosted when people are told that everything is going according to plan, or that to reach a team goal by a dead-line we all need to put in a little more effort. Information, however, should not be used by Christian leaders to manipulate people. It should always be truthful, be communicated with courteousness, and be shared only because we want God's best for those to whom we are delivering the information. Christian leaders should also be open to receive information from those they lead, i.e. be willing to listen and, therefore, to practically show that they care and want the best for the people they lead.

- Making sure that the various areas of church/organisation work are always improving and meeting their goals. People like to be associated with something that is working, improving and successful. This is only possible, however, if the workers themselves are willing to improve/grow/mature in their work for the Lord and in their relationship with Christ. A regular check of the accomplishments, needs and difficulties will be beneficial both to the worker and to those who lead them. Remember, mediocrity tends to only reproduce itself. Church leaders should be able to give their workers clear, well-defined expectations (perhaps worked out with the worker or previous workers) and be able to provide their workers with everything they need to fulfil those expectations. Leaders should also honestly, but sensitively, let their people know where they stand (because people want to know what their leader thinks of them, especially if the leaders reveal this in a positive, upbuilding, trust-creating way).

- Giving more attention and help to team members who are new to a job, and to team members who are not coping well or who are trying hard but not getting very far. These people may need further training, correction, or encouragement. To ignore or embarrass them will often cause these people eventually to stop working hard and to join the ranks of those who do enough to get by. In fact, all team members will need some of their leader's time and undivided attention in order to stay motivated and to encourage their loyalty (e.g. occasionally take people into your office and privately talk with them, asking them questions like 'How are you doing?'). Jesus often motivated His disciples by discipling them personally or in small groups. God's leaders today need to follow Christ's example.

- Encouraging team members to put the Lord first and to spend quality time with Him daily (even in the midst of a busy day). Every day should begin by seeking the Lord, and it is also important at times to put aside our work and bring the Lord into the situation. These quiet times give us time to think, plan and to get things into proper perspective (with the Lord's help). They also help us to make sure we are doing things because they are going to help fulfil God-given team goals and not just for the sake of it.

- Creating an ordered, calm, stable and emotionally safe climate in which the people they lead can grow and be fruitful in Christ. People need to know what is happening and be free from repeated crises/chaos for this to be possible. Of course, they will also need to be challenged and motivated, but it is possible to do this and keep a calm, peaceful environment. A negative, unstable working environment causes people to fight/withdraw or become anxious/apathetic/insecure.

- Making work fun by celebrating birthdays, Christmas, special occasions, any team success etc. Make sure that no one is left out, because to do so would severely demotivate the person. The friendships that a team can bring and the simple fact of people knowing that they belong to a team, are very important motivational aids which should be recognised and encouraged by team leaders.

- Making sure that they do everything possible to enable jobs/tasks to be finished, and that they do not even start ones that are doomed to fail (because this is demotivating/demoralising for all team members). Leaders therefore need to help those people to whom they have delegated tasks, because they are ultimately responsible for those people and their work. Good intentions will never replace good performance as a source of motivation. Jesus finished the task God had set for Him (John 17:4), and so should those to whom God delegates leadership/works of service.

- Helping all team members feel that they have an important, meaningful contribution to make to the team. Leaders need to show their workers how their effort contributes to the overall team effort. Remember, the people around you will all want to be part of the success you, as leader, are creating. Most people love to be associated with something which is successful and will do almost anything to be a part of it. Therefore, help your team members to feel that the team as a whole is successful in what it is setting out to achieve.

- Allowing team members the freedom to make mistakes and, thereby, to learn from them. This will help to give team members the courage to take risks, be creative, and take initiative, etc. The alternative to this is a bunch of frustrated, bored, static, unmotivated team members, many of whom dare not take any risks at all, and so cannot live a life of faith. Remember, failure tends to be something which everyone wants to avoid because it hurts. Leaders will not have to worry too much about giving people the freedom to make mistakes, if they have put the right person in the right job.

- Giving people the authority they need to get the job done.

- Allowing people to be and do the best they can. This will involve giving them some room to make decisions and take risks; not stifling them (even when we, as leaders, feel threatened); training them; equipping them with everything they need to do their job; and motivating them when they need it; etc. Leaders should also encourage their people to be committed, because only committed people give their best; and they should want/expect to see results from their team (if they do not see results, something is wrong, because God has called us all to be fruitful for Him, if we remain in Him: John 15:1–16). In fact, leaders should never fail to do anything that will enable the growth and fruitfulness of the people they lead, i.e. they should fight for them, encourage them, and let them know practically that they have their best interests in mind and that they are on their side.

- Never making loose or rash statements, especially if those statements show any insensitivity to the situation. Leaders should always think before they speak.

- Rewarding goals achieved or work accomplished, rather than the amount of time worked. Remember, being busy can easily become the goal that fills the void of purposelessness.

- Bringing appropriate, constructive criticism. When you have to give a criticism, remember to praise the team member and only criticise their work, where possible. Leaders need to point out constructively errors and any corrections that are needed, if they want their team members to be effective for the Lord. To let people get away with things only encourages sloppiness. Team members should be held accountable for what they do and not be allowed to get away with anything unless they have a good excuse. A constructive criticism contains four elements: it leaves the person with an understanding of what they have done wrong; it shows the person how they can correct their mistake/s; it shows the person that they are noticed and appreciated;

and it encourages the person to do better in the future. Remember, when criticising never begin your criticism by pointing out what is wrong, because that will put the person on the defensive, and defensive people do not listen. The best thing to do is to praise the good points of a person's work and say how much you appreciate their effort and ability. When the time is right, shift the conversation to what needs to be done to make things right or to keep them from going wrong in the future. To end the conversation, affirm the person again and offer your help/support. The person needs to know that you still have confidence in them, so make sure that you appropriately encourage them.

- Sometimes coercion is going to be necessary to get a team member to be effective. For example, if someone is being deliberately lazy or careless, it is better to be direct. Explain to these people that they are letting the team effort down (and are therefore affecting other people and not just themselves), and then set them new deadlines to finish their work. Leaders need to realise that sometimes their authority will need to be exercised in order to get things moving. Remember, love and the Holy Spirit need to be in control when this method of motivating other people is used.

- Letting team members know that they have job security, because people are far more likely to be committed to something in which they feel secure.

- Understanding that team members are going to respond to a situation the way they see it. One way to influence a team member's motivation effectively is to help them to get a more accurate view of what reality or the truth of the situation is.

- Taking into account/consideration the bias or prejudices that all leaders have. These need to be assessed/checked to make sure they are accurate. If not, they should be adjusted/changed.

- Be willing to learn from other people (especially the people they lead). Leaders should set up a suggestion box and read what their people have to say (and do something about what they read, when possible and appropriate). No leader knows all the answers, no matter how knowledgeable or experienced they are. There is always somebody somewhere who will know more about something than they do.

- Demonstrating by their behaviour and by what they say that they are confident in their own abilities and confident in those who work for them. Team unity is greatly enhanced when each member has confidence/ trust in all the others (i.e. they believe in each other's personal integrity, motivation, ability, etc.). It is especially important that team members trust, respect, and have confidence in their leader, and that they know their leader has the ability to lead effectively.

Goal setting and motivation

Few people drop dead from exhaustion, but many give up because they are bored/frustrated/discouraged/unfulfilled for too long. One of the most successful ways of getting a person motivated in any activity (whether it is sport, work, hobby, etc.) is to set the person meaningful, realistically-achievable goals (or get them to set themselves some). These goals should be measurable in some way so that people can see their progress and it should be possible for the person to achieve them on their own. It also helps if the person has some meaningful reward built into the goal achievement.

It is best to work out team and individual goals and even work standards with the people involved. To attempt to impose goals or standards that are not mutually agreed upon can be counter-productive and demotivating for the people. The achievement of individual or team goals is far more likely when they are mutually agreed upon.

Personal goals are a major factor in the motivation process. However, society today emphasizes the worth of the individual and their right to make decisions and choose courses of action that will lead to self-fulfilment. Put another way, society encourages people to set themselves basically selfish life goals. We as Christians, on the other hand, are to be selfless and to set goals that achieve the will of God rather than our own will. In fact, Christianity teaches that the only way to self-fulfilment is to deny ourselves and to follow God as His disciple. Therefore, goal setting for the Christian and for the person in the world, of necessity has to be very different. Christians should bring their personal goals into line with the will of God and not just set goals which only meet their own needs, interests and desires. We will look in more detail at this very important topic of goal setting in a later chapter.

Credibility and motivating other people

This is very important when it comes to motivating those people we lead. If we are not credible as God's leaders, then we will be unable to motivate anyone to serve God (let alone serve God more effectively). Credibility and its twin brother, trust, are hard to gain and easily lost. They need to be worked at, because they take time to develop. In fact, it is only as leaders consistently demonstrate trustworthy and faithful lives, that they will gain credibility with those they lead. Remember, if your image is tarnished, it will not only affect you, it will affect everyone you lead and will reflect on Jesus Christ Himself (2 Corinthians 6:3; 1 Timothy 4:16). Those you lead need to see you as a good Christian first and as a good leader second.

God wants to use our human personality to display His person (i.e. Christian leaders should show other people something of Jesus in their life). In fact, God will use this to help His leaders to entice/inspire those people they lead to change to become as He wants them to be. If they see it work in us, they will be far more likely to also surrender their wills to God and allow Him to work change in them. Remember, good leaders communicate values, help people internalise them and enable those they lead to respond to them.

Things that demotivate other people

A long list of things which demotivate other people could be gained by simply looking at the opposite of the things which help other people to be motivated. However, here we will only briefly look at some of the more destructive contributors to demotivation, i.e. poor organisation/management/administration; weak leadership supervision; failure to keep promises; inability to make wise decisions (at times, leaders will have to take risks when decision-making, because not to do so will cause the people they lead to also be afraid of making decisions); poor working conditions; injustice or unfairness (e.g. playing favourites); inadequate resources/tools/help/training to do a job effectively; humiliating or belittling those people we lead (no one wants to think that other people regard them as stupid or incompetent, so never use words like 'lazy', 'sloppy', or 'inept', because they destroy confidence, initiative and self-esteem); criticising those people we lead publicly; bad personal relationships; no job security; not listening to those people we lead; poor or confusing communication; no goal setting; and little encouragement/affirmation/praise/care. There are many other things that can contribute to a loss of motivation in a team (we have looked at many of these in other chapters).

There are some motivation types that work for a time, but can end up severely demotivating people. These are: guilt motivating (i.e. encouraging a person's feelings of guilt to get them to do what we want, e.g. emotionally blackmailing other people by using the 'poor me' technique); fake enthusiasm (i.e. covering over the reality with high sounding words, or trying to whip up enthusiasm by using emotive language, or orchestrating a crowd and using the resulting wave of emotionalism to appeal to the people, etc.); mutual back-scratching (i.e. we will do this for you, if you do this for us); spiritual blackmail (i.e. claim that God has revealed to us as the trusted, God-called leader what the person needs to do and back it up by telling the person that they should not argue with God); or just plain old manipulation (i.e. using other people by getting them to do something against their will that we as leaders want them to do, e.g. by using force of personality/aggression, pushing or driving people, or using a person's fear of being put down or shamed in public. This may be done out of sheer frustration and it may in the end get the job done, but it can result in very bitter, demotivated people). These types of motivational techniques ought to be avoided at all costs by Christian leaders.

Factors affecting a person's motivation to be part of a team

Some factors which must be considered when looking at a person's willingness to be part of a team include:

- the more self-centred a person is, the less motivated they will be to participate in the achievement of team goals.

- the more contact and involvement the person has with other team members, the more motivated they will be to be part of that team and to achieve team goals.

- the more the opportunities for personal interaction between team members increases, the more the team members will change how they feel towards each other.

- the more similar team members are to other team members, the less likely they are to change in attitude/ thinking, and the more likely they are to stagnate.

- the greater the threat of crises to the team, the more likely it is that individual team members will change their attitude.

- there are also many other factors which are outside of the team itself which affect team members and there- fore affect the team, e.g. how the children have behaved just before a team meeting.

Exercises

1.   As a leader, do you reward the right type of behaviour? Do you want loyalty and commitment, but give to those who threaten to leave, while ignoring those who get on with the job? Do you want unity and harmony in your group/team, but spend the majority of your time with those people who complain the most? Do you want good quality work, but set unreasonable deadlines? Do you want long-term improvements, but only encourage those who have short-term answers? Do you want effective teamwork, but reward one team member at the expense of another? Do you want holiness in your people, but encourage sarcasm, gossip and/or criticism? There are many other questions you could ask yourself. Pray about your leadership style and try to determine anything that needs to change in this area.

2.   *'A sporting coach has a key role especially in team games. It is his job to rouse each team member to play with total commitment. He will try to get the team to play together and with real purpose. He helps each individual to fulfil his potential and to fit into the overall pattern of play. He fires his team to perform with that special 'plus' which is more than the sum of its individual talents. Through its coach a team learns to overcome negative thinking and to become success-minded. With a top coach a team begins to believe it can win and therefore usually does. ... Most of a coach's work is done behind the scenes in careful and thorough preparation. ... The battle is in the mind with many Christians. Men who can equip the church for her ministry will be men who motivate Christians. The best leaders are the best motivators. Moving mountains takes faith. But moving mountains is one thing; moving mountaineers is quite another! ... The coach is not an armchair observer. He is a man with his tracksuit on, a man to whom 'paraclesis' is second nature, a man who loves to get alongside his brothers and sisters and urge them on. In so doing such leaders will not only tell us to 'run in such a way*

as to get the prize', but will convince us by their faith and example that we can.'   (Phil Greenslade)

What lessons from these statements can Christian leaders learn? How should the leader regard their team? After reading these statements, have you realised any areas in which you could improve as one of God's leaders?

3.   Do you live a life that motivates other people to serve the Lord? Are your habits and your life-style what God wants them to be, or do they put other people off Christianity? Can you chart the progress of your growth in God over the last few years and can you see progress in those you lead over the same period? What happens to the people who come into contact with you as a result of that contact? What effect do you have on other people? Does your presence refresh those who need encouragement?

4.   Are you serving the Lord with a sense of rest, peace and freedom which promotes faith, and a sense of ability/skill which produces confidence in those you lead?

5.   *'Motivation, like growth, is inherent within people. Hence, the task to the leader is not so much that of motivating others as it is of unleashing and helping to harness the motivation that is already there.'*   (Paul Buchanan)

Is this statement true? What difference should this make to the way we try to motivate other people?

6.   *'Some leaders believe that most people dislike work, have little ambition or imagination, and don't want responsibility. As a result they lead in a way that fits in with their pessimistic beliefs. This type of leader argues that since people are lazy and unco-operative, the only thing they'll respond to is the stern voice of the autocrat – you tell them what you want done and bully them into accepting your ideas. You would certainly never let them share in decision making or consultation. Only the top people should do the planning! Most of the communication is one way – from you down to them, perhaps through a chain of command.'*
(Derek Copley)

Are there leaders like this? Do you lead like this? Should you? Why not?

7. If the people you lead come to you and ask to be helped in the area of self-motivation, could you help them? In what areas do you need to improve as you seek to motivate those people you lead? In what areas could you improve? Are you going to? Remember, most of the initiatives for change and team member growth come from leadership!

8. Do the people you lead and what they do (no matter how small or obscure) really matter to you? Should they/it matter? What are you going to do about how you feel? Do you ask them frequently how they are getting on and then attentively listen to their answer?

If you have enjoyed this book and would like to help us to send a copy of it and many other titles to needy pastors in the **Third World**, please write for further information or send your gift to:

Sovereign World Trust
PO Box 777, Tonbridge
Kent TN11 0ZS
United Kingdom

or to the **'Sovereign World'** distributor in your country.